FRIEDRICH
SCHLEIERMACHER

Makers of the Modern Theological Mind

Bob E. Patterson, Editor

KARL BARTH by *David L. Mueller*
DIETRICH BONHOEFFER by *Dallas M. Roark*
RUDOLF BULTMANN by *Morris Ashcraft*
CHARLES HARTSHORNE by *Alan Gragg*
WOLFHART PANNENBERG by *Don Olive*
TEILHARD DE CHARDIN by *Doran McCarty*
EMIL BRUNNER by *J. Edward Humphrey*
MARTIN BUBER by *Stephen M. Panko*
SÖREN KIERKEGAARD by *Elmer H. Duncan*
REINHOLD NIEBUHR by *Bob E. Patterson*
H. RICHARD NIEBUHR by *Lonnie D. Kliever*
GERHARD VON RAD by *James L. Crenshaw*
ANDERS NYGREN by *Thor Hall*
FRIEDRICH SCHLEIERMACHER by *C. W. Christian*
HANS KÜNG by *John Kiwiet*
CARL F. H. HENRY by *Bob E. Patterson*

Makers of the Modern Theological Mind

Bob E. Patterson, Editor

FRIEDRICH SCHLEIERMACHER

by C. W. Christian

Word Books, Publisher, Waco, Texas

FRIEDRICH SCHLEIERMACHER

ISBN 0-8499-0132-4
Library of Congress catalog card number: 78-65806
Printed in the United States of America

To Betty

Contents

Editor's Preface

Who are the thinkers that have shaped Christian theology in our time? This series tries to answer that question by providing a reliable guide to the ideas of the men who have significantly charted the theological seas of our century. In the current revival of theology, these books will give a new generation the opportunity to be exposed to significant minds. They are not meant, however, to be a substitute for a careful study of the original works of these makers of the modern theological mind.

This series is not for the lazy. Each major theologian is examined carefully and critically—his life, his theological method, his most germinal ideas, his weaknesses as a thinker, his place in the theological spectrum, and his chief contribution to the climate of theology today. The books are written with the assumption that laymen will read them and enter into the theological dialogue that is so necessary to the church as a whole. At the same time they are carefully enough designed to give assurance to a Ph.D. student in theology preparing for his preliminary exams.

Each author in the series is a professional scholar and theologian in his own right. All are specialists on, and in some cases have studied with, the theologians about whom they write. Welcome to the series.

BOB E. PATTERSON, Editor
Baylor University

Introduction

In history nothing is pure beginning, since the historian always finds himself driven beyond every supposed beginning in search of yet deeper origins. Thus, there is no final answer to the question of the origins of contemporary Christian thought. To point to a particular man or movement is not only to ignore what has gone before and shaped that man or movement, but also to overlook the manifold forces which were at work simultaneously. Therefore, every beginning is a relative beginning, and every founder is to some extent a convenient reference point, a marker on the road to tell us that the journey has entered into a new stage.

Yet it is no mere matter of convenience to call Friedrich Schleiermacher the "father of modern theology." By almost any standard, he must be judged among the most significant figures in the history of Christian thought. His role as an initiator of a new age in theology is secure. He not only summarized the theological insights of Western Protestantism for his time, but also set the general directions that subsequent Christian thought would take. He is one of the very small group of

theologians who have given birth, not to a new theology or to a
new school, but to a new era. It has been said that Schleiermacher had no children, only grandchildren. Though no clearly
recognizable school of theology bears his name, he has influenced directly or indirectly all Protestant theology since his
day.

Schleiermacher has often been called the father of theological liberalism. While there is justification for this description,
it is far too narrow. He is bigger and broader than what came
to be called nineteenth-century liberalism. He is to theology
what Kant and Hegel are to philosophy, namely, the turning
point into the modern world. The more familiar one becomes
with the contribution of this incredibly germinal thinker, the
more difficult it is to conceive nineteenth- and twentieth-century
Christianity without him. Not merely theology is in his debt
but the Christian community, for his theology was conceived
and executed always in the service of the faith.

Like most really pivotal figures in intellectual history,
Schleiermacher combined vision, breadth, and creativity. He
saw with unusual clarity that theology must undergo a revolution comparable to that which was reshaping every other
area of European life and thought. Unlike Luther, who became a reformer largely without intending to do so, Schleiermacher's achievements were both conscious and deliberate.
Again, the comparison with Kant is instructive. Just as Kant had
endeavored to free philosophy from the shackles of medieval
dogmatism that it might move into the future, Schleiermacher
undertook to redirect theology into a new era and to lead the
church into the new world that was coming to be. Indeed, he
spoke of himself as "midwife of a new Christianity."

But Schleiermacher had not only prophetic vision; he possessed a corresponding breadth of perspective. Prophets are not
noted for their breadth; it often suits badly with the intensity
of their vision. Schleiermacher's vision, however, included the
realization that theology could never again content itself with
parochial perspectives or choose to ignore broad areas of ex-

perience. It must come to grips with the growing authority of science, with questions concerning the relation of the church to society, and with the challenge of technological change. Yet it must engage all of these aspects of the emerging world in ways essentially true to the Christian faith and its insights. The incredible range of his interests and competence (generally acknowledged only in recent years) is in large measure the factor that continues to engage students of very diverse interests. Whatever question confronts the modern theologian, he is likely to discover that Schleiermacher has been there before him. Indeed, theology since his day sometimes seems to be little more than a series of footnotes on Schleiermacher.

But vision and breadth alone were not enough to open the way to modern Christianity. Schleiermacher also possessed the creativity to bring about the necessary "beginning again." He was able to rethink the older categories of faith in a way that gave them new vitality and proved viable for a century that seemed ready to cast them aside. Schleiermacher's intention was nothing less than a complete reconstruction of Christian theology in the light of current knowledge and of the prevailing state of the church. The extent to which he achieved this intention is impressive. Although much of the specific content of his thought is now dated, its originality and daring is still evident and, behind the romantic rhetoric, his accomplishment remains remarkably fresh and relevant to the theological tasks of the present.

THE STATUS OF SCHLEIERMACHER SCHOLARSHIP

The serious student of Schleiermacher faces a number of difficulties. Not all of his considerable literary production has been published, and even less is available in translation. Schleiermacher scholarship remained unimpressive, even in Germany, for a half-century after his death. Wilhelm Dilthey's biography of Schleiermacher, published in 1870, stimulated a revival of interest. In 1893, English translation of his works began with John Oman's edition of *On Religion: Speeches to Its Cultured Despisers* (*Über die Religion: Reden an die Gebildeten unter ihren Verächtern*). The "first great flowering" (Tice) of Schleiermacher studies took place in the early decades of this century and grew out of the works of such scholars as Johannes Baur, Rudolf Otto, Albert Schweitzer and Ernst Troeltsch. During these years the first significant works on Schleiermacher in English began to appear, the way being led again by Oman.

This first flowering was brought to an end by the collapse of European culture in World War I. The general disillusionment with nineteenth-century life and thought that marked post-war Europe was reflected in the emergence of dialectical theology. "Neoorthodoxy" represented a protest against the dominant theology of the Ritschlian liberal school and, insofar as Schleiermacher was seen to be the chief source of that theology, he became the focus of a major theological reevaluation and the subject of a sustained critique. Karl Barth was perhaps the most subtle and perceptive of the critics of Schleiermacher, while Emil Brunner, in his *Die Mystik und Das Wort*, was a more strident spokesman of "Schleiermacher redaction."

The neoorthodox critique largely dominated Schleiermacher studies through the fifties. Yet it did serve to call attention to him as a crucial source of modern Christian thought. As the impetus and the persuasiveness of crisis theology faded and the questions it had brushed aside reasserted themselves—questions with which Schleiermacher had sought to contend—a new and more sympathetic Schleiermacher scholarship began to appear. Interest in Schleiermacher has reached at present a high level and shows no sign of abating.

The reader who wishes to pursue the study of Schleiermacher further should secure Terrence N. Tice's excellent *Schleiermacher Bibliography with Brief Introduction, Annotations and Index*,[1] an exhaustive documentation of Schleiermacher research through 1964. Tice has also provided a modern critical translation of Schleiermacher's *Über die Religion: Reden an* *die Gebildeten unter ihren Verächtern,* employing the title *On Religion: Addresses to Its Cultured Critics.** In addition, we are indebted to him for translations of two other writings essential to an understanding of Schleiermacher's theological development—*Christmas Eve: Dialogue on the Incarnation (Die Weihnachtsfeuer: Ein Gespräch)* and the *Brief Outline of the Study of Theology (Kurze Darstellung des theologischen Studiums).* For a sensitive intellectual biography, the reader is directed to Martin Redeker, *Schleiermacher: Life and Thought.*

Several excellent scholarly treatments of Schleiermacher have emerged in recent years. Perhaps the writings of Richard R. Niebuhr stand out. His *Schleiermacher on Christ and Religion* is of special interest, as are his several articles and his brief introduction to the Torchbook edition of *The Christian Faith (Der Christliche Glaube nach den Grundsätzen der evangelischen Kirche in Zusammenhange dargestellt).* Gerhard Spiegler's *The Eternal Covenant* gives special attention to the relation between Schleiermacher's philosophical *Dialectic (Dialektik)* and *The Christian Faith.*

A word remains to be said about the approach to Schleiermacher's thought to be taken in the following pages. The primary intention of the book is to present in readily available form the basic substance of Schleiermacher's theology. Because of the unique significance of his thought as the first major theological response to the challenge of the modern world, it is of special importance that the nature of that challenge be understood and that the fundamental problems with which he wrestled be made clear. A portion of chapter one is devoted to giving preliminary attention to the cultural and intellectual background of Schleiermacher and the nineteenth century.

It should be noted also that the present study is largely limited to Schleiermacher's specifically religious writings.

---

* All references to the *Speeches* in the present study are to the Tice translation unless otherwise specified.

While it is important to understand the theology of Schleiermacher against the broader range of his scholarly interests, the scope of the present book precludes any thorough examination of his nonreligious writings, except where references are necessary to clarify his theological method and content. The Niebuhr and Spiegler works and the fine intellectual biography by Martin Redeker mentioned above are recommended to the interested reader who wishes to pursue this area of study.

In the final analysis, Schleiermacher was first and always a theologian, and a theologian in the service of faith. His labor in other disciplines was ancillary to and served the needs of his effort to give to faith a new expression for his time, and it is almost entirely as a theologian that his impact is to be felt today.

The primary aims of the present book are:

1. *The exposition of the main lines of his theology.* Through the first half of the twentieth century, Schleiermacher's stature as a thinker often was obscured by the polemic of neoorthodoxy against liberalism; his theology could not be understood or appreciated until his place in the broader scope of modern thought had been examined. Most recent scholarship has concentrated on such an effort, and it is now possible and appropriate to begin to examine his theological work on its own terms. This volume will focus attention on his major theological writings. In the last analysis, Schleiermacher's impact on the Christian world still rests on the *Speeches on Religion* and *The Christian Faith.*

2. *The clarification and critical evaluation of his thought.* The contemporary reader of Schleiermacher faces many difficulties, some of which result from seeing him too long through the eyes of his critics and some from problems inherent in his method and in his theological system itself. Much of the text will be directed toward clarifying these difficulties.

3. *The projection of lines of basic influence.* Schleiermacher's unique position in the history of modern theology requires that an effort be made to assess his significance. Because

of the complexity of his thought, we can do no more here than to suggest broad lines of influence, and these only in the most obvious or significant areas. Nevertheless, we will seek to achieve some sense of the deep debt that the theology of our time owes to F. D. E. Schleiermacher.

I. The Man and His Times

A WORLD ABORNING

Ever since the late seventeenth and early eighteenth century, a profound alteration of culture has been taking place which John Randall has called "the making of the modern mind." Its roots are deep in the past, but it began to manifest itself in the Renaissance and then appeared with a new vigor and coherence in the last half of the seventeenth century. After 1650 a number of cultural, historical, and intellectual factors combined to produce a world view very different in important respects from that in which the Christian faith had emerged. It was also significantly different from the partly biblical, partly Greco-Roman culture that was dominant during the Middle Ages. Like all beginnings, this outlook was evident at first in an isolated few. By the eighteenth century it had captured the majority of the intelligentsia of Europe and, since then, it has increasingly saturated the whole of Western society.

This new world view, largely secular, scientific, and optimistic in outlook, confronted Christian faith with a challenge of major proportions. Virtually none of the presuppositions of traditional theology remained untouched. The history of modern theology is largely the story of the church's attempt to come to terms with the emerging outlook and to renew the dialogue with the world that had been broken off by the decline of medieval-Reformation civilization. The church at the dawn of the nineteenth century found itself asking how it was to restructure its message so that it would be meaningful to modern men and, at the same time, remain faithful to its historic confession—in other words, how was Christianity to gain the world without losing its soul? Nineteenth-century liberalism, in all its varied expressions, was the first sustained effort to confront this challenge and to make Christian faith viable in the modern world. The cultural and social changes that produced the modern mind were exceedingly complex. However, certain elements of the new mentality provide the background against which Schleiermacher's thought must be understood.

1. *Enlightenment rationalism.* The ferment that produced the modern world became evident in the age now known as the Enlightenment.[1] In the eighteenth century, western Europe, emerging from the chaos of the religious wars, began to make rapid progress over its long-prevailing natural and social problems. The result was a great burst of optimism and confidence in the power of man to master himself and his universe. The tool of this mastery, and therefore of progress, was seen to be human reason. Man could overcome the past and create the future if only he could restructure his world by the power of his own mind. Autonomous reason became the primary criterion of truth: nothing could be accepted as true that could not be grasped and verified by the free operation of the mind.

The challenge of rationalism to Christian faith was beginning to be felt by the end of the seventeenth century, but the depth of the crisis it represented was not evident at first. Early Enlightenment rationalism tended to be deductive—that is, it sought to understand reality through the unfolding of truth by means of self-evident axioms revealed in the laws of logic. Since deductive rationalists were logicians and system-builders, their thought had much in common with the great systems of medieval theology and philosophy. As the eighteenth century progressed, the practical sciences gained influence by demonstrating their potential for functional utility, and their empirical, experimental methodology became increasingly the pattern for all knowledge. Thus the rationalism of the eighteenth century became steadily less deductive and more inductive, finding its truth not in self-evident propositions but in the conclusions it drew from concrete experience. Empirical reason, unlike deductive reason, quickly proved to be a powerful acid, dissolving the meticulous systems of the past. For faith, the potential trauma inherent in the Enlightenment lay, first of all, in the triumph of the empirical principle, for it seemed to cut the ground out from under most of the basic affirmations of traditional theology. In a world that judges by the criterion of sense experience, where does one turn for evidence of God?

Enlightenment rationalism did not represent a crisis for faith at the theoretical or methodological level only. The problems of epistemology were of little concern to the practical shapers of eighteenth-century society. It tended also to create a distinctive set of attitudes foreshadowing the modern age and in significant conflict with many of the basic attitudes of medieval and Reformation society. For instance, while medieval society lived out of its traditions, with its values rooted in the stable soil of the past, the Enlightenment represented a revolt against the past in the name of human progress and on the grounds of autonomous reason. "Enlightenment," said Kant, "means think for yourself." The corollary of reason is freedom from all externally given dogma. Thus, all values depending on appeal to authority alone were called in question, and this included, of course, the authority of the church.

Suspicion of authority did not mean only past authority; it included any claim to truth not given to all men everywhere. If reason was the universal possession of all men, then nothing could be true that was not, at least in principle, available to mankind without reference to time, place, or tradition. One often detects in the spokesmen of the Enlightenment a sense of having risen above the pollution of history into the calm, clear air of universal truth.

As the principle of "the universality of truth" cut through the shackles of tradition and opened the way to change, it provided much of the dynamic for social and technological progress, but it once again presented faith with an awesome challenge. The church rested its claims not only on the authority of the past but on truths received from God by special revelation, enshrined in tradition and Scripture, and available nowhere else. In the face of the principle of universality, how could a theology with such roots lay claim to the confidence of men? Could one really believe eternal truth to be the possession of a single Semitic tribe in Palestine and their elect successors? But if faith no longer could be defended on the basis of the sacred writings and traditions from the past, on what basis could it be defended? Or, if tradition was to speak with vigor in a new day, how could it be made to recover its voice?

The ease with which the Enlightenment dismissed the authority of the past revealed its growing confidence in the moral integrity of man. Rational man was man under control, and therefore good. Social evil was viewed largely as a remnant of an irrational past. Man, freed from the tyranny of tradition, had within his grasp the power to control not only physical nature but even the baser elements of his own nature. Reinforced by the very real progress of the previous century, a confident humanism emerged, setting a tone that persists in large measure into the present.

The new understanding of man as good, rational, and self-sufficient cut across the grain of medieval, and especially Reformation, anthropology. The eighteenth century viewed as repugnant and socially paralyzing such ideas as original sin and the bondage of the will. Much as empiricism had called into question the truth of Christianity, the self-sufficient humanism of the Enlightenment challenged its practical necessity. Religion no longer seemed to be needed as a basis for human values or as a hedge against evil. Indeed, in view of the questionable record of Christian society in the past—and particularly the bloody religious wars of the previous century—many concluded that religion, especially revealed religion, and most particularly the Christian religion, was the chief enemy of inquiry and social progress.

2. *The dethronement of God and man: developments in the special sciences.* The empiricism of the Enlightenment implied not only a new view of man, but also of nature, one radically different from that in which Christianity had taken shape. The Christian faith was born in a milieu partly Hebrew and partly Greco-Roman in character. Though not identical, these perspectives had certain elements in common that allowed them to coalesce in classical and medieval culture. Above all, they agreed that the world was inherently purposive and that man was included in its purpose. The Aristotelian-Ptolemaic universe was geocentric and, since man was the sovereign of earth, anthropocentric. Man belonged to the purpose of creation, and human values had a "home" in reality.

Beginning with the sixteenth century, developments in the special sciences began to create a very different picture of things. All the lines of scientific progress converged to call into question the central place of man in creation and the purposive activity of God in the world. The nature of the crisis was made progressively clearer by developments in the physical sciences. As early as the sixteenth century, Copernicus had undermined the traditional geocentrism of Aristotelian-medieval astronomy, removing man from the physical, and thus also the psychological, center of things. And every subsequent development seemed to underscore the insignificance of man. Older cosmologies had placed him at the focal point of nature and history. Now, increasingly, it seemed impertinent to think that the universe was concerned about man.

The dethronement of man by astronomy was an accidental result of scientific discovery. The subsequent disappearance of God from the cosmos was a direct result of the principles of rationalism. Empirical rationalism made it increasingly difficult to speak meaningfully of nonphysical realities and non-immanent causes. Furthermore, the principle of universality required that all attempts at explanation, whether of phenomena in nature or events in history, appeal only to evidence both universally and publicly demonstrable. Together, the principles of empiricism and universality made all reference to divine activity in the world increasingly problematic. It remained for Newton to elevate these rational principles to the level of methodology by demonstrating that all phenomena in the physical world were susceptible to explanation by a single, immanent, universally applicable principle: magnetic attraction, or gravity. With the establishment of this principle, God was pushed to the periphery, being replaced as the active reason for the facts of the world by finite causality. If he remained at all, it was as the remote cause of the system as a whole.

3. *Time and the Scriptures: geological uniformitarianism.* Despite the subtle displacement of God and man in the scheme of things, most sciences before 1750 did not clearly challenge the biblical perspective. Primarily structural rather than genetic, premodern sciences sought to describe and classify nature but were not greatly concerned, as the Bible seemed to be, with origins.

While all the sciences began to develop genetic interests with the awakening of the nineteenth-century historical consciousness, it was the relatively new science of geology that led the genetic revolution. Uniformitarianism, the governing principle of the new geology as formulated by Hutton and popularized by Lyle, was the basis of the revolution. This principle was nothing more than the application of Newton's law of uniform causality to time and was the logical extension of the principle of rational universality.

The result of uniformitarianism was the projection of a new geologic history in which the earth was understood to be formed by natural forces over a relatively vast time span. The consequences of this new perspective for traditional faith were chiefly two:

(1) For the first time, science confronted belief not with a structure but with a history. Structural science and biblical history had been able to coexist. The scientist described nature as it displayed itself in the present; the Bible explained how it came to be that way! Now biblical religion was faced with a science whose basic methodology was historical. It sought to answer questions about the present order and structure of the world by investigating the origins of that order. In the process it projected a very different view of world origins from that presented in Genesis, and this new view had the ring of truth. The trustworthiness of the Bible, at least in important areas, seemed to be undermined.

(2) The dethronement of man was deepened further. Whereas the Copernican revolution had reduced human existence to a mote in space, geology seemed to reduce human history to a wink in infinite time. Instead of finding himself in a world created as his cradle ("Time," said one writer, "is only six days older than we"), man was confronted with endless ages in which life-forms had come and gone in aimless fashion, and in which human life had appeared only in the last brief moment. Would he also go, as he had come, in an endless river of cosmic history?

The extension of the developmentalism of Hutton and Lyle to biology was a foregone conclusion. It was also to prove the ultimate shock to the human sense of meaning in the universe. The impact of *The Origin of Species* lay in the fact that Darwin destroyed the final bastion of man's sense of significance in nature: his biological uniqueness. As long as humankind could be viewed as a special creation, different in kind and in manner of origin from the rest of nature, man could preserve his sense of purposive existence even in the face of a seemingly purposeless nature. Darwin's was not the first blow but the last: his theory seemed to plunge man into the chaotic order of nature.

The cumulative effect of the process described above was the calling into question of many of the basic presuppositions on which Christianity had stood; for example, the providential activity of God, the value and importance of man, the trustworthiness of the Scripture (on which belief in God and man rested), and the structure of human values that had undergirded Christian civilization.

4. *The birth of historical awareness.* Most of the modern sociological sciences were born out of the Enlightenment, and each has had an impact on Christian thought. None, perhaps, has been so far-reaching in its effects on the modern mind as the science of history. The nineteenth century was the century of history; after 1800 all sciences and disciplines became historical. Among many reasons was the discovery of the development of the cosmos by astronomy and geology. More immediately influential was the growth of knowledge about other cultures. The growing familiarity of Western society with other societies made evident the historical origins of customs and institutions. It also stimulated interest in the processes by which they had been shaped.

The rise of historical consciousness had a varied impact on Christian faith and thought. Insofar as it awakened interest in the traditions of the Christian past, it was to provide much of the dynamic for positive theological reconstruction during the next century and a half. Indeed, historical theology as a recognizable discipline hardly can be said to predate Schleiermacher. In at least two important respects, however, the crisis confronting faith was deepened by the outlook and methods of historiography:

(1) *The application of historical, critical methods to the Scriptures.* It was inevitable that the Bible would be subjected to examination by the new methods of historical research being applied to other historical sources. Such examination proved devastating to ancient assumptions regarding the historical inerrancy of Scripture. Furthermore, since the principles of historical research were shaped largely within the

context of the natural sciences, the historical study of the Scriptures often led to a profound skepticism regarding those elements of the Bible not compatible with naturalistic presuppositions, for example, miracles.

The historical study of Scripture raised serious questions about the factuality of the life of Jesus and made it hard for Christians to feel confident about the "truth value" of affirmations based on that historicity. Thus historical science seemed to threaten the tenuous connection of faith to its origins. Much of nineteenth-century theology had at its heart the historical question so central in Schleiermacher's little masterpiece, *Christmas Eve*, namely, how can we affirm the truth of Christian doctrine when the historical events to which it points have been placed in doubt?

(2) *The problem of relativism.* In a historical order every event is limited in space and time, and every perspective on truth is partial, colored by the point-of-view of the beholder. What then is the meaning of absolute truth—of final revelation—in a world where every conviction rests on the parochial perspective of the viewer? On what can confidence and human values rest if no truth can make a claim to finality? Perhaps the most persistent problem for religious faith from Schleiermacher to the present has been what Heinz Zahrnt has called "the end of all certainty." [2] While the relativity of knowledge was not without its positive values for theology (it made possible a new humility and therefore a new graciousness among theologians) its visceral impact was to deepen further the crisis for faith begun by empirical rationalism and the physical sciences.

Thus the world aborning confronted faith with a fundamental crisis of authority. How can the truth and significance of religious faith be validated in the light of empiricism? How can they be validated in the light of historical relativism? The history of Christian thought since 1800 is in large measure the attempt of faith to find answers for these questions.

SCHLEIERMACHER AND THE NATURE OF THEOLOGY

Schleiermacher's significance for modern theology lies to a great extent in the clarity with which he perceived the challenge for faith described above and the honesty with which he sought to respond to that challenge. Others reacted to the crisis with equal vigor but, because they lacked his breadth of perspective, or because they were less than clear about the issues involved, their achievements remained fragmentary or one-sided. The shape that the theological enterprise assumed in his understanding and the actual character of his own theology, molded by that understanding, indicate the clarity of his intention. Some preliminary comments regarding Schleiermacher's perspective on the nature of theology will serve to delineate his stance as mediator between the church and the world aborning.

1. *Theology is experiential.* Schleiermacher represents Christian faith awaking to the challenge of empiricism. From his earliest writings, Schleiermacher is emphatic that no future theology could be validated by appeal to authority alone. Theology must acknowledge the demand of the modern mind for evidence derived from experience. He understands, of course, the narrowness and the superficiality of that brand of scientific empiricism that purchases simplicity at the cost of reality. He has little patience with the reductionist mentality that cannot penetrate beyond the obvious and therefore lives by the rule of "nothing but." Such "wretched empiricism" he ruthlessly exposes in the *Speeches.* Schleiermacher is empirical, but in a broader sense—in a sense that today might be called phenomenological or existential. He has no use for theological or metaphysical speculation that cannot be rooted in the primal soil of human experience.

To speak of Schleiermacher today as an empirical theologian is to invite real misunderstanding. If the term *empirical* cannot be divorced from a narrow sensationalist context, then perhaps it would be less confusing to speak of his thought as experiential. But whatever designation we use, according to Schleiermacher all thought is rooted in experience, and *theological* thought grows out of *religious* experience—especially the corporate experience of the worshiping community. Nor does it, once generated, take on a life of its own, independent of its origins, as if it were the task of the community to discover timeless truths and set them free. Theology must return ever again to its origins in the lived faith of the church. The search in the *Speeches* for the "really real" in religion is never a search for an abstract essence, but for the living reality that shapes expression and thought. Indeed, a search for an experiential foundation for faith is evident in all of Schleiermacher's theology.

2. *Theology is historical.* Schleiermacher's thought is not merely Christian thought become empirical; it also represents an awakening of historical consciousness. He is the first major theologian to become thoroughly historical in his understanding of life and thought, and yet to remain a loyal son of the church. He is fully aware, for good or evil, that theological thought must be redefined in terms of history. His historicism is explicit. Even a cursory examination of his writings makes evident what Richard R. Niebuhr has called his "intense preoccupation with history," [3] and renders even more inexplicable the criticism frequently made that he is a subjectivist concerned only with a timeless dimension of intuitive awareness—with the soul in mystic communion with God.

His profound grasp of the historical character of thought determines the questions Schleiermacher puts to faith—for example, the question of how a nineteenth-century Christianity, immersed in modern thought forms and separated from its roots by centuries, could recapture its past, comprehend that past, and relate it to the present. This question is not only the central concern of the *Christmas Eve* of 1805, but also of his lectures on biblical hermeneutics. In this respect, Schleiermacher anticipates the hermeneutical preoccupation of modern theologians, a concern that arises in a similar way from the historical problem described above.[4] Just as there is no abstract self apart from the world, so there is no thought that escapes the relativity of time and place—not even the seemingly absolute truths of the experimental scientist or the deductive rationalist. But for Schleiermacher, the consequences of relativity are not all detrimental to faith and truth. Relative truth is also *truth in relation*. If the fact of relativity dooms us to less than final truth, it also opens to us a new appreciation of the rich and dynamic possibilities of understanding inherent in the shared life of historical existence.

3. *Theology is communal.* Schleiermacher's grasp of knowledge as historical frees him to take more seriously the communal character of faith and to understand the way in which theology must, in the last analysis, be the creation of the worshiping fellowship, not primarily the work of the religious genius. Theology is always *church* theology, and the theologian is ever the servant of the church. Furthermore, insofar as the church is historical—that is, insofar as it is not a dead past fact but a living, changing organism—then the dogma it creates is dynamic, requiring new expression with every generation.[5]

4. *Theology is confessional.* Insofar as theology's task is to give expression to the faith of the church, it is also confessional. It may derive its logic from philosophical dialectics, but its substance is rooted in the experience of faith. The theologian speaks from within faith or he is in fact no theologian.[6]

5. *Theology is pastoral.* Theology is more than confessional. While it arises from faith and seeks to give coherent intellectual expression to faith, its driving force is not intellectual, nor is its primary function the service of "scientific" knowledge. The task of theology in its philosophical, biblical, and historical forms, is to serve the practical needs of the worshiping community. The usual separation of the roles of minister and theologian is, in Schleiermacher's view, unfortunate: theory without practice is finally pointless, and practice without theory is blind.

Although practical divisions of labor are necessary, Schleiermacher sees the ideal leader of the church as a "thinking pastor." Indeed, the persistence with which he himself pursued a preaching ministry throughout his career and the active role he took in shaping the affairs of the German church show how deep was his commitment to this ideal. One who knows how to do theology in the service of the community he calls a true "Prince of the Church." [7] Terrence Tice expresses it: "Dogmatics is the scholar servant of proclamation in all its forms: of preaching, but also of the whole vast field of Christian action covered by ethics and practical theology." [8]

6. *Theology is systematic.* Theology is not merely confessional and pastoral; it is also systematic. As the scholar servant of preaching, dogmatics must be true not only to the experience of faith but also to the requirements of clear thought and to the rest of life within which the church exists. Theology not only must express the faith out of which it arises (this Schleiermacher calls its "ecclesiastical value") but it must also achieve internal coherence. It cannot escape the requirements of logical consistency simply because it is dogma. It seeks to give expression to the insights of faith in such a way as to make them understandable and, at the same time, to demonstrate their relationship to the rest of knowledge. (This inner coherence and outer relationship Schleiermacher calls the "scientific value" of theology.) [9] Theology, then, to be valid for the living community of faith, must be (1) recognizable by the church as its own ("This is really what we feel and know and confess!") and (2) intelligible ("What we confess makes sense!"). To be systematic, Schleiermacher contends, theology must bear its witness to the whole of life and truth. [10]

7. *Theology is ontological.* Schleiermacher fully understood the dilemma confronting the theologian and every other searcher for truth. Once the historicity of understanding has been granted, can knowledge be saved from solipsism and subsequent despair? Even appeal to the communal character of knowledge has limits. Such an appeal may provide an element of personal reinforcement, but a shared opinion or a common

tradition gives only a temporary shelter from the cold. The most congenial confessing community must finally ask if its confession is true.

Although Schleiermacher could never accept the retreat from history implicit in the transcendental idealism of Fichte and Hegel, he could understand their asking about the transcendental grounds for historical truth. Thus Schleiermacher understood what many of his critics among the crisis theologians have not understood: that the confessional nature of theology must not blind the reader to its ontological interests. For Schleiermacher, finally, that alone can be the basis of the living community which by its very nature points the faithful beyond existential origins to its essential ground in God. Every theology of experience must ask, explicitly or implicitly, about that reality which makes possible any experience at all.

Schleiermacher, because of his historicism, was a critic of arrogant and often empty speculation, but this should not obscure his commitment to a kind of realism that does not, like empty idealism, ignore the concrete, dynamic unity of particular being. Speculative idealism thus "annihilates the Universe, while it seems to aim at constructing it." [11] Philosophy and theology seek not to construct imaginative fables but to speak of that which is finally real. Schleiermacher, as will be indicated subsequently, was a cautious metaphysician, but he was a metaphysician nonetheless.

THE SHAPING OF THE MAN

Friedrich Daniel Ernst Schleiermacher, born in 1768 in Breslau, was the descendant of three generations of Reformed ministers. His father, a Prussian court chaplain of somewhat deistic tendencies, experienced in 1778, while under the influence of a Moravian community at Gnadenfrei, a renewal of personal faith and resolved to educate his son in the Moravian environment. It was at Gnadenfrei, in 1783, that Friedrich underwent the religious awakening which he described in later years as the beginning of his awareness of a "higher order." The same year he was enrolled in the Moravian School at Niesky. The religious impact of Niesky was to be lasting. Although Schleiermacher subsequently revolted against the obscurantist theology of the Brethren, he retained a deep regard for their sincere piety and warm personal faith and could, in later years, refer to himself as a "Moravian of higher sort." His abiding distaste for the sterility of rational religion and his feeling for the worshiping community as the real locus of religious thought have Moravian overtones.

He began his formal theological training at the Moravian Seminary at Barby in 1785. There he first became acquainted with elements of Enlightenment theology, albeit in polemic form. There also he was touched by the early stirrings of Romanticism. He read Goethe's *Werther* and began to move away from the mild "world-contempt" of the Moravian anthropology toward a modified humanism. His move to Halle in 1787 expressed his resolve to break away from the restrictions of Brethren life and thought and precipitated a painful rupture of relationship with his father. At the University of Halle, from 1787–89, his intellectual horizons broadened. Here he encountered the critical theologies of Wolf and Semler. Most important for his future development was his encounter with the philosophy of Kant. By 1788 he had achieved, largely by his own efforts, a thorough grounding in transcendental philosophy.

The years at Halle were years of intellectual growth, but they were difficult years for him with regard to his own religious life. He found himself sinking into skepticism and self-doubt. Redeker calls the winter of 1789/1790, spent at Drossen, "the lowest point in Schleiermacher's personal history." [12] It was also during these years that he became convinced of the essential religious sterility of the rationalist Enlightenment theology which he briefly espoused under the thralldom of Kant.

His recovery from skepticism began in 1793. After passing his initial theological examinations, he took a post as tutor in the home of Count Dohna of Schlobitten. The impact of this remarkable family was deep and lasting. Here an atmosphere warm and congenial, coupled with a conservative but open and intelligent Christianity, transformed the young man. Here began to develop his understanding of friendship as that which makes possible the actualization of true freedom and individuality by binding men to each other in true community. He speaks eloquently in the *Soliloquies* (*Monologen: Ein Neujahrsgabe*) of the time when "in a stranger's home my sense for the beauty of human friendship was first awakened." [13]

It also seems likely that an important insight took shape at Schlobitten to influence his understanding of the relationship between faith and its theological expression. Schleiermacher discovered while with the Dohna family that differences in the formulation of faith did not necessarily mean differences in its substance. Despite the significant gulf between the conservative theology of the count and his own Enlightenment theology, he came to understand the bond of faith that united them as well as how individual expressions of faith grow out of a shared common reality. This discovery, on the one hand, allowed him to value each differing expression of the shared life for its own sake and, on the other hand, to seek for the inner essence from which it flows. Schleiermacher writes:

> Amid all the diversities of this world's motley spectacle I learned to discount appearances and to recognize the same reality whatever its garb, and I also learned to translate the many tongues that it acquires . . . to look into the inner nature of things.[14]

It is not surprising that, in this congenial setting, the young theologian's own religious life was reawakened and he began to preach. In 1794 he took a pastorate in Landsberg and in 1796 became chaplain of the Charité Hospital in Berlin.

The six years in Berlin were crucial ones for Schleiermacher, beginning what Redeker calls the first intuitive and creative period in his activity as a theological and philosophical thinker.[15] He became involved in the cultural and learned circles of the city, and especially the romantic coterie headed by Friedrich Schlegel, who became a close friend of the young chaplain. Out of this association came the publication in 1799 of what even today remains his best-known writing, the *Speeches*, a brilliant enterprise in religious apologetics. A year later it was followed by the *Soliloquies*. During this period he also undertook, at first with Schlegel and later alone, a translation of the *Dialogues* of Plato, which was to have far-reaching influence on his mature thought.

After 1800 it became evident to Schleiermacher that he was not akin in spirit to the Berlin group. His romantic ardor cooled, and he began to develop his thought with a new seriousness and systematic rigor. His departure from Berlin to a small pastorate at Stolp marks the beginning of his maturity as a thinker and theologian.

Schleiermacher's academic career began in 1804 when he became professor at the University of Halle. Although he continued to be active in the pulpit and in practical church and public affairs, from this time forward his primary labors were in the university. At Halle the range of his scholarship became evident as he lectured on hermeneutics and ethics, and developed the substance of his philosophical *Dialectic*. Among the theologically important works of the period is the remarkable little Platonic dialogue *Christmas Eve*.[16] Prepared in 1804 as a Christmas gift for friends and published in early 1805, this meditation on the Incarnation gives expression for the first time to many of the insights that inform *The Christian Faith*.

In 1809 Schleiermacher was called to participate in the organization of the University of Berlin. As dean of the theological faculty it was his task to structure the theological curriculum. The program he designed was given the title *Brief Outline of the Study of Theology* when it was first published in 1810, and serves as an excellent introduction to his subsequent works. *The Christian Faith* first appeared in 1821/22.

Revised in 1831/32, only two years before his death, it is beyond question his finest accomplishment and one of the most significant theological achievements of modern Protestantism.

Since Schleiermacher was uncommonly sensitive to the social and intellectual currents of his day, the formative influences in his thought are manifold. Certain of the more significant forces shaping his theology demand brief comment:

1. *Moravian influences.* Schleiermacher's religious life and his early theological understandings took shape in the midst of Moravian pietism. The tone set by those years remained in all of his mature thought. Of the elements of the Moravian faith that left permanent imprint on the young theologian, the most obvious was his association of religion with feeling. Furthermore, Schleiermacher, like the Moravians, attributed the awakening of religious feeling not to the initiative of the believer but to the free action of God—in other words, he viewed religious awareness as depending upon and arising from grace.[17]

It is surprising how often superficial evaluations of Schleiermacher fail to grasp the profound sense of grace that suffuses his whole theology. Intellectually, of course, Schleiermacher's theology of grace owes a debt to his Reformed heritage and to Augustine, but its personal roots seem to be Moravian. Whatever its source, his sense that everything of value in one's consciousness of God—everything that can rightly be called religion—comes as "gift" is very deep. Indeed, Schleiermacher's well-known definition of religion as the feeling of absolute dependence is perhaps best understood as the awareness of the utter "givenness" of faith. Schleiermacher was a theologian of grace. It is this sense of grace that often prevented him from slipping into the easy social meliorism that was to characterize so much of the liberalism of subsequent generations, and of which he often has been accused. Schleiermacher was never Pelagian.

Another persistent Moravian element was the sense that Christian faith arises from a deep, personal devotion to Jesus.

The "Jesus piety" that is expressed so poignantly in *Christmas Eve* and renders Schleiermacher's mature theology so consistently christological, seems to have taken root in Moravian soil. He early broke with the Moravian literalistic theology of sacrificial atonement but retained a deep sense of the centrality of "redemption through Christ," a theme that provides the definitive structure of the third part of *The Christian Faith*.

2. *Immanuel Kant*. Schleiermacher read the *Critique of Pure Reason* and the *Critique of Practical Reason* (then new) as a student at Halle. The impact of Kant was pivotal in determining his future course.[18] Apart from contributing to his deepening religious skepticism at the time, Kant's influence was more methodological than substantive. Schleiermacher accepted the basic conclusions of the critical philosophy concerning the limits of speculative knowledge. Confronted with the force of Kant's metaphysical agnosticism, Schleiermacher felt compelled to forego the metaphysical task in its traditional sense. In fact, the chief value of Kant's philosophy for Schleiermacher in his later years was its usefulness as a tool for tearing Enlightenment theology away from its rationalistic moorings. Schleiermacher's major philosophical work, the *Dialectic* of 1805, has been described as Kantian both in its method and its resultant metaphysical and theological agnosticism.[19]

But while he found the master of Koenigsberg useful for clearing away the debris of rational religion, Schleiermacher was never truly Kantian in spirit; Kant could not provide him with a basis for the reconstruction of faith. Schleiermacher felt that the religious object as constructed by Kant on the postulates of practical reason was no more recognizable to the worshiper than was the god of sterile rationalism or the "absolute" of speculative idealism. It was inevitable that Schleiermacher would seek to get beyond the limits imposed on experience and knowledge by both extending and criticizing Kant in the direction of a new "realism." The intention to transcend Kant's skepticism is present in the *Speeches*, and so to some extent is the achievement, but the theoretical foundation for such a "higher realism" took shape only after his confrontation with Plato.

3. *Romanticism.* To analyze the relationship of Schleiermacher to the Romantic Movement is difficult, in view of the amorphous character of romanticism itself. To speak of Schleiermacher as the theological expression of romanticism is ambiguous at best. Further, since "romantic" is used in theological circles today as a word of opprobrium, to call Schleiermacher a romantic is to bring him under suspicion. In his biography, Redeker adopts the expedient of limiting the term to a narrow circle within Berlin literary idealism. But this does not really help, because the Berlin romantics were a part of a wider outlook that shaped them and Schleiermacher as well.[20]

Insofar as the term *romantic* refers to a shallow and noncritical aestheticism, a kind of vacuous religiosity devoid of intellectual rigor and integrity, Schleiermacher was no romantic. Indeed, he was among the most vigorous critics of such an approach to life and faith. His relation to the Fichtean idealism of the Schlegel circle was more complex. He shared their suspicion of the analytic approach to reality and their longing to discover the underlying unity at the heart of reality, but in many ways he was never completely at home there. That he could not accept the thoroughgoing idealism of Fichte, with its stress on the creative activity of the Ego, was evident from the beginning. He felt that Fichte had insufficient feeling for the individual, and thus tended to allow concrete selfhood to be submerged in the infinite reason.[21] It is chiefly Fichte who is the target of the scathing words of condemnation directed at "vain speculation" throughout the *Speeches.* For Schleiermacher, that striving arrogance which seeks to achieve God by speculation—which indeed *creates God*—is a far cry from the true religion which humbly receives God as grace.

The influence of F. W. J. Schelling was perhaps more abiding, especially in Schleiermacher's tendency to define the Ultimate as the unity of the antitheses of existence. However,

Schleiermacher refused to identify the transcendental unity demanded by *thought* with *being*, thus constituting it an epistemological rather than a metaphysical necessity. He sought to stay clear of the dilemma toward which he felt the idealists were moving, namely, the construction of a "philosophy of identity" whereby finite creation is swallowed up in an all-encompassing and featureless whole.[22]

In what sense, then, is it correct to call Schleiermacher a romantic? Insofar as romanticism represented a partial reaction to the increasingly cold, analytical, and technical reason of the scientific mentality and a corresponding attempt to rediscover the rich unity of life behind "appearances," Schleiermacher was a son of romanticism. By the beginning of the nineteenth century, the feeling was widespread that Enlightenment reason—Kant's pure reason—was a very good way to know but a very unsatisfactory way to *live*, that it was incapable of dealing effectively with the relations of life or of grasping the nature of reality as a dynamic, living whole. Rationalism was analytic, while life was organic, and so many of the dimensions of experience that bestowed on the world its color and vitality seemed inaccessible to empirical reason. Romanticism was, at least in part, an effort to recover a deeper dimension of life, often by appeal to imagination and intuition as supplementary routes to truth and understanding.

For Schleiermacher, romanticism confirmed his belief in the basic unity of life and provided the standpoint for his criticism of Kantian religion in the *Speeches*. It also reinforced certain deep convictions remaining with him from his Moravian days. For instance, his sense of community and his belief that personal identity arises from the relationships of family and human fellowship were affirmed by the romantic stress on the individual as a part of the organic whole. Schleiermacher's distaste for the artificiality of rationalistic religion and his deep love for the flawed but concrete communities of worship had roots in this dual Moravian-romantic heritage. Perhaps his romanticism is evident most clearly in his sense of the dynamic

unity-in-diversity which constitutes the world, wherein individual and community, the organic and the inorganic, the universal and the particular are bound to each other in creative
tension and in which each takes on its identity through relation
to the other.

4. *Plato.* The significance of Plato for Schleiermacher has
not been sufficiently appreciated. Failure to recognize the deepening Platonism in the mature thought of Schleiermacher was
one of the main reasons subsequent generations of theologians
misinterpreted his intentions, even while claiming to be his
disciples. This same failure of understanding is at the root of
the charges of subjectivism hurled at him with such persistence
by the sons of Albrecht Ritschl in our own century. Plato's influence was both methodological and substantive.[23] He helped
Schleiermacher perfect his own philosophical and theological
method by providing a model for his still inchoate understanding of the "dialogic" and communal character of truth.

Furthermore, Plato in large measure prompted the change
in style that characterizes the mature works of Schleiermacher,
a change to a careful and systematic rigor of expression, sup-
pressing the rhetoric of persuasion that dominates the *Speeches*
and the rhetoric of aphoristic self-revelation in the *Soliloquies.*
Perhaps most important, the Plato studies coincide with the
decline of Schleiermacher's metaphysical agnosticism and the
emergence of a strain of realism marking his mature theology
(the "higher realism" he reached out for in the *Speeches?*).
Henceforth the search for the essence at the heart of faith—for
the "really real" in religion—becomes more explicitly ontological. The common judgment that he reduces theology to
subjective human experience must be qualified, since for Schleiermacher experience and the reality reflected in and required
by it cannot be separated. Thus in *The Christian Faith,* God is
not available merely as a necessary postulate, derived from
and secondary to the experience; he is given *in* experience. To
have the feeling of absolute dependence is the same thing as
to be in relation to God.[24]

Schleiermacher seems to have felt after 1805 an increasing confidence that faith can pursue its course toward knowledge. It is true that he continued his polemic against speculation, but his attack was directed toward those who seek to generate actuality speculatively. Schleiermacher, at least after Berlin, recognized the inevitability, and even the necessity, of "speculation." He demonstrates again and again in *The Christian Faith* that faith must extrapolate from its primordial consciousness the conclusions demanded by it. What he objected to was irrelevant speculation, or especially idealistic speculations that claimed to provide abstract and certain knowledge untouched by the realities of experience and the exigencies of practical life. He was, in a way that Hegel and also many of Schleiermacher's critics in the present century are not, a conscious and honest philosopher. His violent protestations in the two open letters to Lücke [25] that he had never allowed his theology to be shaped by any philosophy must not be understood to mean that the idea content of an honest theology—that is, one which is an honest expression of a genuine faith—has no truth value. His Platonism would not let him escape the realization that a speculative entailment of experience is more than a postulate, so that if experienced reality has no *fundamentum in re*, then the experience itself is stilled. For instance, to feel absolutely dependent, and then to refuse to acknowledge the actuality which is the referent of that feeling, is to render the experience itself absurd and ultimately to destroy it.

In effect, Schleiermacher had discovered what Jonathan Edwards concluded in his critique of Locke, namely, that every positivism whatever (even confessional theological positivism) demands a metaphysic. Henceforth Schleiermacher would insist, in Niebuhr's words, that "appearance is grounded in the thing itself." [26] Niebuhr comments, "[Schleiermacher's] kinship to Plato on this architectonic plane enables him to transcend his period and stand with such men as St. Augustine, John Calvin, and Jonathan Edwards who similarly combine a pathos for ultimate reality with a profound understanding of the moral nature of man." [27]

It is not an exaggeration to say that Plato provided Schleiermacher a way back into a confessionalism that did not need to take refuge in obscurantism. Because of his sense of the historicality of all thought, he could rest lightly on his metaphysics and yet acknowledge that faith points to something real and of ultimate concern.

II. The Speeches on Religion:
A Quest for New Beginnings

The question confronting Schleiermacher and nineteenth-century theology was whether it was any longer possible to restore the vitality of Christian faith and to provide a basis for a vigorous and creative future. The double crisis of scientific empiricism and relativizing historicism seemed to tear away the foundations on which traditional Christianity had stood. Claude Welch has expressed the two absolutely urgent questions which confronted the generation of Schleiermacher; namely, whether theology is any longer possible in the modern world, and, even if it is, whether a *Christian* theology is possible.[1] Schleiermacher's work as a theologian can be understood in large measure as a response to these questions.

If the rehabilitation of faith and theology was to be more than doctrinaire, several specific demands faced the one who assumed the task. First, he must find a new authority for faith, since the traditional appeal to church authority and Scripture seemed no longer sufficient. Second, he must demonstrate how the work of theology is to be done in the changed intellectual and cultural atmosphere of the modern world. Finally, he must show what an adequate theology—one which is at the same

time truly modern and genuinely Christian—has to say. Thus
the theological quest of Schleiermacher is threefold: it is (1) a
search for authority, (2) a reconstruction of theological
method, and (3) a reformulation of the content of religious
faith in general and of the Christian faith in particular. All
three of these concerns are reflected in Schleiermacher's first
major publication, *On Religion: Speeches to Its Cultured
Despisers.*[2] It is the first of these concerns—the search for a
new authority—which dominates this brilliant but immature
work. Many of the insights which would inform his mature
theology appear for the first time in the *Speeches*. However,
the way from the theology of the *Speeches* to the mature
theology of *The Christian Faith* is rarely direct, for the intuitions of 1798 had to pass through profound modifications
before they achieved the form that could accurately be called
"Schleiermachian."

THE *SPEECHES* AND THE SEARCH FOR AUTHORITY

The *Speeches* burst upon an unexpecting world in 1799. The
author was then thirty-one years of age and a member of the
romantic coterie of Henriette Herz and Friedrich Schlegel in
Berlin. The fact that Schleiermacher published at all we owe to
Schlegel's insistence. Schleiermacher felt he did not share in
full measure the creative impulse evident in some members of
the group. The *Speeches* and the *Soliloquies,* published a year
later, are the effort of the young preacher to find a "voice"
with which he could speak. The peculiar character of the
Speeches—neither sermonic nor scholarly—reflects the nature
of his relationship with the romantic set. His sense of ministerial vocation made him an anomaly in his circle of friends
and eventually drove him from their midst. Nevertheless, it
was in this setting that he began to discover his special gifts
as a "virtuoso of friendship," and it was as a mediator—between religion and its cultured despisers—that he wrote the
Speeches.

The book is a brilliant work; its daring, originality, and sustained creativity are still impressive. But it is also an immature work. The insights regarding both the method and substance of theology which were to shape Schleiermacher's thought often wrestle together like Jacob and Esau in the womb. The difficulty for the modern reader is partly the fault of the high romantic rhetoric, of which Schleiermacher was not a master, but the problems are not entirely stylistic. In their sometimes embryonic state, the ideas do not achieve that clarity and precision of expression so praised by Schleiermacher himself in *The Christian Faith.*

Despite the sometimes diffuse and incomplete nature of the *Speeches,* it continues today to be the most widely read of Schleiermacher's published works and possibly the best-known work by a theologian of the nineteenth century. Because of its pivotal role in modern theological history it deserves to be well known, but it is unfortunate that it has overshadowed Schleiermacher's later writings. Considered alone, the *Speeches* gives an unsatisfactory picture of the overall stature and contribution of the author, yet much of the polemic directed at Schleiermacher by neoorthodox theologians seems to rest almost exclusively on this work.

A word is in order concerning Schleiermacher's audience. It is generally agreed that the *Speeches* are addressed not to the totally hostile critics of religion or to the indifferent masses, but to those within the literary and artistic community whom he knew in Berlin—people who, like himself, remained sensitive to the deeper dimensions of life to which faith always had pointed, but who had concluded that human community and value could be achieved without reference to traditional religion and to God. In addressing these "cultured despisers," Schleiermacher was at one level delivering his justification for his ministerial vocation. But beyond this, he hoped to enlist them in an assault upon the true enemies of a vital and creative faith, namely, the shallow and superficial natural religion that was the theological consequence of Enlightenment criticism and the empty utilitarianism that was its practical expression. Because these cultured despisers retained their feeling for the deeper dimensions of reality, Schleiermacher felt they were capable of understanding, if properly shown, the failure of the one and the sterility of the other. If they could be made thus aware, they would be open to a new and better understanding of what they intuitively valued.

The general aim of the *Speeches* is twofold. First, Schleiermacher seeks to disarm the critics of religion by demonstrating that what they have rejected is not religion in its truest sense, and that their stereotyped attacks for the most part have been misdirected. Therefore the polemics against religion that his hearers find so persuasive will be seen to be directed at straw men of their own creation, leaving real religion unscathed. Having accomplished this first ground-clearing operation, he seeks to reconstruct religion on a new foundation that will resist efforts to render it irrelevant to life.

Such an awesome task demanded a new point of departure. If a generation was to be saved from agnosticism or indifference, on what basis was such a rescue possible? The older theologies had started from revelation—from a sacred book, the truth of which rested on authority. Now science had cast doubt on the authority of Scripture. Furthermore, men seemed committed to the empirical principle and skeptical about any claim to truth unable to make appeal to verifiable evidence. On what basis was one to speak a word for God to the sons of Kant?

The direction taken by Schleiermacher in the *Speeches* represents nothing less than a Copernican revolution in theology. If men are persuaded only by what they encounter in their own experience and by what the sum of their rational judgments confirm, then no other point of departure seems to offer itself than the concrete fact of existence. One must confront life itself and seek to discover in it some dimension that points to the validity and, one hopes, the necessity of religion. Thus Schleiermacher turned to an empirical justification for faith—

or, if not empirical in the narrow positivistic sense, at least experiential. Henceforth the truth of God and religion would rest on the testimony of the self in the deepest recesses of its own being, and nothing could be affirmed finally as true and meaningful without the confirmation of the heart.

The appeal to "religious experience" that characterizes theological liberalism has its roots in this revolution, and it accounts for the tendency of later liberals to talk more about religion than about God, since religion is the immediate and empirically available datum. It is, of course, this turning to a quasi-empirical or experiential basis for the rehabilitation of religion that has been viewed as the tragic error of nineteenth-century theology. This is not the place to consider whether experiential theology is equivalent to subjectivism and whether an anthropological methodology predestines an anthropocentric religion. Certainly Schleiermacher intended no such abandonment of the objective grounds of faith—not in the *Speeches* and most certainly not in *The Christian Faith*. The question is whether in 1800 there was any workable alternative, and whether there remains any alternative today. However strident the protests of dialectical theology against the "subjectivism" of Schleiermacher, it can hardly be said that Barth has avoided the necessity of appealing finally to the "affirmation of the heart." It was certainly clear to Schleiermacher, and remains clear to anyone who takes Kant seriously, that whatever the objective data with which the mind deals, it is experienced in and appropriated through the subject.

The acceptance of this subjectivist principle by Schleiermacher and his contemporaries had a profound implication for future theology. When combined with the growing historicism of the modern mind and its concomitant relativism, it made increasingly evident the confessional character of all theology. Insofar as the authority for religion and for doctrine is in the religious subjectivity of the believer, it can function as an authority only for and within a community of experience. If there is no experience that men share, then there is no escaping religious solipsism. In such a case communication ceases and religion is reduced to mystic silence. Insofar as communities of experience exist, however, the lonely subjectivity of the believer is ratified by the worshiping community; thus his solitary subjectivity is taken up into and reinforced by the subjectivity of the group.

The discovery of a shared awareness of faith provided something at least comparable to the public character of truth required by scientific empiricism, and yet was compatible with a becoming modesty regarding other claims to truth as embodied in other communities of faith. Within a community a common awareness of God is affirmed, and the primary function of theology is not to defend that common awareness against other views of the world or of God, but rather to give expression to the faith of the community and to strengthen it in its life of worship. For Schleiermacher, then, theology is always theology of and for the church. In this regard, the confessionalism assumed by such later liberals as Ritschl and Herrmann and which becomes so explicit—even polemic—in Barth is part of the legacy of the *Speeches*.

What are the questions to which the *Speeches* are addressed? Rudolf Otto's summary makes clear with what unerring instinct the young Schleiermacher goes to the heart of the crisis confronting religious faith:

> What is religion? How does it arise? How does it emerge in history? What are religions? What is Christianity? What in religion is valid in a "natural" or "positive" sense? What is the meaning of a religious community? . . . What is the relation of religion to moral behavior? to knowledge? What are the conceptions and teachings of religion (that is, what is theology and doctrine) and do they have any validity? [3]

Each of these questions is examined in the *Speeches*. The course of the argument is determined by Schleiermacher's basic goals: (1) to clear the ground by demonstrating that the idea of religion his hearers have rejected as irrational and nonempirical is a false idea; (2) to redefine religion in terms identifiable with their experience—that is, to make religion once more thinkable; (3) to argue that religion so defined is not merely one value among others, but the very foundation of all values and the basis for the unification of life; (4) to demonstrate that the reality of religion requires and, indeed, creates fallible but positive communities of faith (in other words, to show why one cannot have religion without religions); (5) to examine the relationship of religion in general to Christianity (a task made necessary by the growing awareness of world religions); and (6) in the process of answering these questions, to explain, reinterpret, and "demythologize," if you will, many of the basic categories of religious and Christian thought so as to make them comprehensible to a new age. If these goals can be reached, Schleiermacher feels that he will have begun the journey toward a completely contemporary and yet honestly Christian theology.

THE DIALECTIC OF EXISTENCE

On what could a defense of religion be based? Since there were few a priori assumptions about God and religion shared by Schleiermacher's readers, and since what assumptions they did make about religion were largely misguided, a deductive argument was not possible. Furthermore, the inductive mentality of the time seemed to demand that all claims to truth be empirically grounded. It was equally evident, however, that the narrow empiricism of the natural sciences was of little use, because its sensationalist methodology and materialist presuppositions precluded on principle the very "data" to which appeal had to be made. The method, therefore, that Schleiermacher adopts in the *Speeches* can best be described as phenomenological. He seeks to analyze and describe experience in such a way as to elicit recognition.[4] In the first two speeches, entitled "Defense" and "The Nature of Religion," he seeks to discover an aspect or dimension of experience to

which he can point as the universal ground of piety, and to
show it to be the source and object of all religious devotion,
howsoever varied in particular expression. His intention is to
strip away all the accompaniments of religion in order to discover its essence—"the religious in religion" [5]—which is the
source of the worship life of mankind.

Schleiermacher begins his task with a psychological analysis
of human existence.[6] Contemplation of the natural world, he
suggests, reveals a bewildering multiformity in which, nevertheless, each particular is bound to the rest in a dialectic tension. Two moments coexist in everything that is: a moment of
individuation, in which the entity is seen in all its unique particularity, as over against the "multiverse," and a moment of
participation in the whole of being. These two moments are
held in creative tension in every positive existent. The dialectic
of individuation and participation manifests itself in human experience as the awareness of self and world. The relation of the
self to the world is twofold. There is a passive aspect in which
the world flows into the self, shaping it and giving it its substance; there is also an active aspect, in which the self acts
upon and determines the world. Insofar as the world gives itself to us—"in-fluences" us—we *know* the world. Insofar as
we act upon the world, we determine it in freedom; therefore
we *do*. We are acted upon, and we also act; we are determined
and we are free. We are what we are by reason of the world,
and the world is what it is at least in part because of our
activity. Thus our primary datum of consciousness seems to
be the dialectic of knowing and doing. We are never merely
objective observers, but subjective shapers; we are not merely
rational beings but also volitional beings.

This dialectic of life to which Schleiermacher points is
the basis of the dualism that has characterized epistemology
from the Eleatics to the present day, and that had assumed the
proportions of a crisis in the century and a half from Descartes
to Kant. Most of the dualities characterizing Western thought
reflect this dialectic: objectivity and subjectivity, isolation and

involvement, the individual and the social nexus, knowing and doing, science and art, pure reason and practical reason, metaphysics and ethics. If, then, these two dimensions of experience are the true sources of all science and art (and after the two great critiques of Kant, which of Schleiermacher's hearers would doubt it?), to which does religion relate? What is the place of religion in the Kantian scheme? Is religion a kind of knowing or a kind of doing? Does it consist of truths about the world, or is its essence to be found in the realm of moral activity?

RELIGION AS KNOWLEDGE OF GOD
AND THE WORLD

Religion, Schleiermacher insists, is *not* knowledge. Indeed, the present crisis of religion is derived in part from the error of thinking it so. Schleiermacher sadly observes that religious and nonreligious thinkers seem to agree in considering religion a body of knowledge, a collection of observations or a system of theories about the nature of the world, its functions, and its ends (that is, creation, providence, and eschatology). Certainly it had come to be understood this way in the eighteenth century. What was deism but "those ill-assembled fragments of metaphysics which people now call 'purified Christianity' "? [7] Indeed, had not Christian theology of all ages contributed to this error by failing to distinguish between the propositions of faith and the deeper sources from which they flow?

Religion as metaphysics—as truths about the world—has serious liabilities, however. It is nonempirical, at least in the narrow sense, and always obliged to defend itself before the bar of pure reason. In most recent attempts it has come away in disgrace. Religion as a system of truth is, furthermore, lacking in inner consistency. It has often been self-contradictory and in the modern world it has been proven to be, quite simply, wrong. It is, in short, bad physics and bad metaphysics.

But religion in its true nature is not knowledge. It has an idea content, to be sure, but to mistake it for its idea content is to make a category error. The thought content of a religion is its external expression, not its essence. To know religion is to discover the deeper source from which its doctrines flow.

It should be noted that the distinction Schleiermacher makes here between the essence of religion and its doctrinal and conceptual expression was to become an important one in the development of subsequent theology. The distinction, so familiar in liberal Christianity, between the "kernel" of religion and its "husk," between "abiding truths" and "changing categories" (Fosdick), as well as the distinction between the symbols of faith and the reality from which they spring (Tillich), would have made little sense before the development of the modern historical consciousness. Yet it is doubtful whether a modern Christianity, with its awareness of confessional and theological multiplicity, could have developed without it. By recognizing that the theological expression of religion was not identical with religion itself, Schleiermacher opens up a way of escape from the unbearable burden of defending all past religion and doctrine by frankly acknowledging the particularity of dogma and practice without thereby losing the truth at their heart. The recognition that there is a distinction between the eternal substance of religion and its historical manifestations, including those of Christianity, is a first step beyond the dogmatic past. That this step was necessary if Christian faith was to come to terms with the modern world seems to have been demonstrated by the history of theological development in the last two centuries.

Schleiermacher argues that a fair consideration of religion as a living phenomenon will dispel the illusion that it is identical with its ideas. Is it not evident to all that when a person is most deeply immersed in religious reality—when he is *being* most religious—he is least conscious of the ideas commonly thought to be its substance, for instance, God, freedom, and immortality (Kant)? Furthermore, when a person is engaged in worship, is he learning new content? Conversion is scarcely a lecture on God. Indeed, if religion had to do with knowledge, then it could be imparted by instruction and the most learned man would be the most religious—and this is patently absurd. Increase in knowledge does not entail an increase in piety.

RELIGION AS MORAL ACHIEVEMENT

If religion is not a kind of knowing, what other possibilities exist? Perhaps it arises from the other pole of the dialectic; perhaps it is a kind of doing. If religion cannot be preserved as true knowledge, perhaps it can be justified as essential for moral conduct. Kant himself had located the sphere of religion in the practical reason, and many who had given up religion as a source of truth were willing to defend it as a way of living. However, the keener spirits of Schleiermacher's day saw clearly that the morals of the religious were not always good and—what was more significant—that a moral existence was possible without religious sanctions.

Although there is a special intimacy between religion and the practical, creative dimension of the soul (and therefore with its manifestations in art, ethics, culture), its essence is not practical. Indeed, while morality and ethics, as well as artistic creativity, are all essentially active in character, religion is characterized more truly by passivity. The awareness that informs every meaningful act of art or morals is freedom over against the world—freedom to act upon and to change that world. The tonic awareness of worship is not freedom but dependence. Nor does the moment of devotion exist for the sake of its practical expression, however truly it gives rise to practice. It is its own goal. We do not worship in order to be better men, although we are better men because we worship.

To assign religion to either of these spheres—knowing or doing—in exclusion of the other, would compromise its relation to the whole of existence, and would perpetuate the tragic separation of the world of fact from the world of value begun by Descartes and continued by Kant. It is a measure of Schleiermacher's creativity that he refused the dualism of fact and value that became such an attraction to the Ritschlian tradition. If the moment of religious awareness is not essentially intellective, neither is it ethical.

THE ESSENCE OF RELIGION

If religion belongs neither to knowing nor doing, it must be *sui generis*. It must have its own sphere, a third dimension of the soul, independent of the others and in a certain sense prior to and more basic than either. But what remains? Ironically, Kant himself may have provided the clue upon which Schleiermacher seized. In a lesser known work, the *Critique of Judgment*, Kant attempted, not too successfully, to do justice to a third form of human awareness that seemed not to fit well into the body of the critical philosophy, namely, the aesthetic consciousness. Here was an area as native to experience as the pure and the practical reason and incapable of being reduced to either. Man is aware not only of the true and the good, but of the beautiful as well. He not only knows and does, he also feels. Here, in the realm of feeling, according to Schleiermacher, lies the essence and the source of religion. He writes: "To seek and to find this infinite and eternal factor in all that lives and moves, in all growth and change, in all action and passion, and to have and to know life itself only in immediate feeling—that is religion." [8]

At last, then, emerges the formulation that more than any other is associated with Schleiermacher's name: *religion is feeling!* But great care must be taken if we are to avoid the mistake so often made of seeing the *Speeches* as an undignified retreat into emotionalism. While this error is partly Schleiermacher's fault—his vision is cloudy and his choice of words leaves much to be desired [9]—it is also the fault of later generations that failed or refused to hear him carefully. What does he intend to say?

Schleiermacher's choice of feeling as the area of experience most akin to religion reflects, as noted earlier, his years among the Moravians, whose warm piety he still valued, and also the dissatisfaction with sterile rationalism that he shared with the romantics. His reasons for the appeal to feeling are thought out carefully. He does not, of course, mean that religion is to be equated with emotions or that to feel deeply is to be religious. Emotions are unstable and highly variable and are, furthermore, conditioned by finite objects and experiences— that is, by the world of knowing and doing. Schleiermacher is trying to point beyond the particular feelings that ebb and flow to the deeper ground of all feelings in the awareness of personal continuity and unity—that is, to the abiding consciousness of selfhood.

In the psychological trinity of knowing, doing, and feeling, it is clear that feeling has a certain priority. It comes first genetically, the infant evidently having an active and powerful life of feeling before the intellective and moral faculties develop. But feeling is also, one might say, *morphologically* prior. The others exist in varying degree and are to some extent mutually exclusive, but some feeling—some effective tone—accompanies every state of being. Indeed, insofar as the flux of intellectual and volitional experience can be seen to cohere at all, it is by virtue of the unifying of the self in feeling. To clarify his meaning, Schleiermacher seeks to lead his hearers behind the ordinary awareness of self and world: "We shall endeavor to descend into the innermost sanctuary of life. . . . There alone you may discover the original relation of intuition and feeling from which alone this identity and difference is to be understood." Since thinking is discursive— that is, since it operates at the level of the dialectic, and "thought can embrace only that which is sundered" [10]—the deeper unity of life to which he points can be awakened only by poetic evocation on his part and sympathetic participation on the part of his hearers.

The several attempts at defining religion in the first two

speeches reflect different dimensions of religious awareness. Religion, viewed subjectively, is a "sense and taste for the infinite." [11] With reference to the rest of creation, it is "the universal being of all things in and through the infinite, of all temporal things in and through the eternal." [12] Furthermore, since religion intuits not merely the self and the world but the profound unity in which both self and world exist, true piety is not merely awareness of self or world—not even awe at the majesty of creation. It includes such awareness, but it contemplates the works of creation and is moved by every particular thing—"not for its own sake but as a part of the whole . . . as a representation of the infinite in our lives." [13]

Finally, a true intuition of the infinite carries with it an awareness of indebtedness and dependence. Schleiermacher's impatience with the transcendental egoism of Fichte is evident in the early *Speeches*. Fichte shows how far he is from true piety in his Promethean confidence that man's world of meaning and value is his own creation. The pious man knows that he is not the ground of his own being—that all comes to him as a gift, flowing from the great unseen reality in which all things cohere. In other words, religion at bottom is grace. Thus Schleiermacher can conclude:

> The sum total of religion is to feel that, in its highest unity, all that moves us in feeling is one; to feel that aught single and particular is only possible by means of this unity; to feel . . . that being and living is a being and living in and through God.[14]

Thus the primary goal of the *Speeches* is made manifest. By demolishing his hearers' delusions about the nature of religion, Schleiermacher feels he has opened the way for a second step. He believes the way is clear to show why religion, so understood, is not only real but also essential to the integration of life in its various dimensions. His argument thus far may be summarized as follows:

1. Religion arises from our felt awareness of our depen-

dence on the source of all things—God—and therefore includes
our sense of unity with all that is real.

2. Since the root of religion is givenness, religion is essentially passive. Its original movement is one of receiving,
and the emotional tone is that of dependence—or as Redeker
puts it, the feeling of humility and creatureliness, of awe as
opposed to sovereign power.[15]

3. Religion, as has been shown, is neither thought nor action—indeed, the worshiper in the moment of ecstasy is little
concerned with dogma or moral precepts—but it is the ground
and source of both. Religion drives toward understanding in
that the pious heart seeks to unify in *thought* what it feels to
be one in reality. Religion also tends toward moral activity
by giving rise to a human sympathy and by generating a longing for more complete unity with God and with his creation.

4. True piety, then, is the basis of the wholeness of selfhood
in all its dimensions. Here rests the ideal integration that
determines the quality of the rational and practical life and
sets the tone of individual and corporate existence. Thus it is
the mother of every other unity. Only a healthy faith can
prevent the breaking down of life into conflict and fragmentation, into war between a cold, impersonal intellect and a
fanatic, activist will. Religion, then, is not only the necessary
concomitant of personal wholeness; it is the reality that, properly understood, could rehabilitate a disintegrating culture.
Kant had bequeathed to the modern age his own bifurcated
world, split hopelessly between pure and practical reason, between the scientist and the poet. Thus the ancient vision of the
wholeness of life had been lost, and Schleiermacher's age
found itself banished from the land of unity. Only a society
which had lost contact with its primal sources could tolerate
such splitness and believe that people could have "right knowledge without right conduct and vice versa." [16] True religion
supplies the principle of unity which alone can heal the splitness of the modern world.

RELIGION AND GOD IN THE *SPEECHES*

The first two speeches contain the central argument of the
work. Schleiermacher confidently concludes that, as a result of
his defense, religion is untouched by its critics, and, further,
that it is essential to truth and wholeness in man and in society.
Without it, life remains unreal and incomplete.

The publication of the *Speeches* brought forth immediate
acclaim and criticism. The nature of the work, the frequent
imprecision of its language, and the novelty of its formulations
generated serious questions. Some of these continue to figure
in contemporary discussions and demand attention in any attempt to evaluate Schleiermacher's significance as a Christian
thinker:

1. *Do all men have a sense of the infinite?* Schleiermacher's
argument seems to assume the awareness of the divine, however muted, in all men, at least insofar as they are capable of
wholeness as selves. Since all men are equally creations of the
"World-Spirit," it is difficult to imagine a human being without at least a dim awareness of the givenness of his being.[17]
Indeed, he is convinced that "there are none to whom the
sublime Spirit of this world has not appeared at least once,
casting a piercing glance upon them . . . which the downcast
eye senses without directly seeing."[18] Man then is *homo re-
ligiosus*—religious man. At times the reader of the *Speeches*
might even suspect that, by virtue of the presence of the infinite in all things, a person could rise to religious awareness
by enhancing this native endowment.

Schleiermacher can indeed urge upon his hearers the necessity of awakening in themselves the sense of the eternal that
lies sleeping. But his rhetoric of persuasion must not mislead
us. Already in the *Speeches* Schleiermacher has set himself
against the easygoing and arrogant Pelagianism of Enlightenment religion. To intuit the divine is to know that we have that
intuition as a gift, and that in no sense have we stirred it up

by our own contemplative or practical powers. Thus the most
powerful corrective to the shallow self-confidence of Enlightenment religion is the intuition of true religion. To be aware of
the Infinite is to know that it *comes to us*. It is not our creation,
but we are creations of the Divine, and the proper response is
awe and reverence. Neither can we choose to turn by our own
power and become disciples and believers—"No one can enter
at pleasure." [19] The awareness of the presence of the Infinite
in the finite is, once again, describable only by the language of
grace. "The Universe forms its own observers and admirers." [20]

2. *Is the Schleiermacher of the* Speeches *a pantheist?* The
charge of pantheism does not surprise the casual reader of the
Speeches. Quite apart from noting Schleiermacher's praise of
the "atheistic" Spinoza,[21] one wonders why God appears so
seldom in the work. And why, instead, is the religious intuition
associated so intimately with the intuition of the world? The
language of the *Speeches* is problematic if Schleiermacher
does not intend to identify the Divine with the totality of the
world. What is religion, he asks, but a sense and taste for the
Infinite in the finite, communion with the Universe, fellowship
with the "World-Spirit"?

Despite the suspicions aroused by such language, Schleiermacher steadfastly resists the accusation of pantheism, and
a careful reading of the *Speeches*, especially in the light of the
second edition and of the notes appended to it, tends to support
his protest against the charges.[22] He reminds his critic of the
apologetic intent of the *Speeches* and suggests that his terminol-
ogy arises in large measure from a desire not to alienate pre-
maturely those who would be uneasy with "God-talk." Indeed,
his sermons of the same period, addressed to a different audience, have a more theistic tone. Yet his choice of language is
not mere accommodation. Schleiermacher recognizes the valid
instincts that inform classical pantheism (where it has not
become a subterfuge for a collective materialism), instincts
made all the more forceful by the emergence of the scientific
world view. The pantheist understands that nothing exists in

and of itself. In that sense, it is God's presence in everything that makes it *be*.

He also understands that there is no knowledge of God that is not mediated through finite reality. Thus any experience of God is at the same time an experience of the world. This fact, for Schleiermacher, had been made more evident by new knowledge of the causal structure of the physical world. Negatively expressed, there are no "extraordinary" events of revelation that violate the order of nature. Positively put, insofar as God is to be known, he must manifest himself through the events and objects of the world. But to know the Divine in and through the world is not to know merely the world, even in its overwhelming majesty. Religion is not awe for "big finitude"; [23] it is awareness of the mystery on which the world itself depends. God is in the world because he is the ground of its being, but he is not identical with the world.

One implication for such an understanding is that the progress of science need no longer be seen as a threat to religion. Faith does not rest on the mystery of the unknown, which could be dispelled by more knowledge, but on the mystery that illuminates the known. Religion, properly understood, is not awe at what we do not understand, but at what we *do* understand. God does not need the gaps to make himself known, and the fear—made explicit in modern times by Dietrich Bonhoeffer—that science is the death of mystery is groundless. Mystery confronts us not only in the obscure but also in the lucid.

A second implication of this insight—that God is mediated through his world—is that the ordinary objects and events of the world are all, at least potentially, capable of revealing God. There is no object or event that cannot be a sacred shrine, no place that cannot be holy ground. There are, to be sure, certain experiences that are especially suited for mediating the divine—"windows to the infinite," he calls them—but in principle nothing can be excluded. Nothing is profane in and of itself. All nature and history are sacramental and can be the instruments of God's self-manifestation.[24]

But despite its valid instincts, pantheism is in error, and its error lies in its identifying God with the world. Schleiermacher's primary reason for rejecting pantheism is religious, not theoretical. Pantheism fails to understand that the physical universe itself is involved in the dialectic of life, is itself a world of tension and antithesis, and requires a deeper unity. Even big finitude is finitude, and its reason for being is not in itself. Put in terms of his mature theology, we can never feel for the world what we feel for God, that is, absolute dependence. To confess God is to confess that reality on whom we depend for our very being, but who, in turn, does not depend on us. We feel no such dependence on the world. Our dependence on the world is very great but far from absolute. It conditions us massively; we condition it trivially but truly. Thus religion itself is the best critic of pantheism. Faith directs itself not toward finite multiplicity but toward that unity which enfolds multiplicity and transcends it infinitely. Only this is God.

3. *Is the God of the* Speeches *nonpersonal?* The question of Schleiermacher's relation to traditional theism is more difficult. It is clear that Schleiermacher is uncomfortable with personalistic descriptions of deity. He maintains that a theistic understanding of God is not essential to religion. This he feels is evident historically. Are there not religions that lack such an understanding? It is also evident to Schleiermacher from his personal history. Indeed, one of the touchstones of his own religious life was the discovery that faith could survive even the death of its own icons. He recalls in the *Speeches* a time when "the childhood images of God and immortality vanished before my doubting eyes."[25] Perhaps he is referring to the year at Drossen when his uncritical conceptualizations began to crumble under the impact of Enlightenment criticism. His most telling discovery was that, though he could rid himself of those now inadequate conceptions, the dimensions of experience

to which they had referred, and from which they had in large
measure arisen, persisted. He found that the reality survived
the death of the concept and gave rise to renewed conceptualiza-
tion. In Paul Tillich's language, the symbols died, but the
reality to which they pointed survived and gave birth to new
symbols.

Thus Schleiermacher learned that God is not to be confused
with *ideas* about God. Yet faith requires expression, and poor
or inadequate formulation can inhibit faith. Therefore if God
is not to be banished along with unworthy ideas about God—
and the older theistic ideas with their uncritical anthropomorphism seemed to Schleiermacher no longer tenable—then a
vigorous effort must be made to transcend them.

Schleiermacher's struggles in the *Speeches* anticipate a century and a half of subsequent debate about God. He recognizes
the inability of personalistic language to exhaust the substance
of religious awareness and to escape the absurdities that were
driving modern men to skepticism. He is especially fearful of
any description of God that undercuts God's character as the
power behind and in all things. The peril of conceiving God
as a being among other beings is religious, not merely theoretical. A God so conceived is "drawn down into the region
of opposition," into the dialectic of life where everything
causes and is caused alike. Such a God is no longer the power
of all things and the ground of all being, and the religious
instinct itself is contradicted. Therefore, those who revolt
against such naïve anthropomorphism are not without religion
or God for doing so. Schleiermacher expresses sympathy with
the person who conceives of God "not as personally thinking
and willing but as comprising that general necessity which is
exalted over all personality, which brings forth and conjoins
all thought and being." [26] It is not surprising that the *Speeches*
prompted charges of atheism, or that reputable scholars have
pronounced Schleiermacher's God to be the anchor of a philosophy of identity. [27]

But Schleiermacher also is aware of the inadequacy of nonpersonal descriptions of God. A nonpersonal idea of God is still an *idea,* and as such it also is finite. Furthermore, insofar as it is a *human* idea, it is anthropomorphic.[28] In reacting to naïve, sensuous anthropomorphism, we run the danger of creating a more sophisticated, though vacuous, kind. If personalistic theism tends to naïveté, nonpersonalistic ideas of God tend to be abstract and religiously empty, corresponding in small degree to the living reality of which the believer is aware in moments of true worship. "Just look at how limited the representation of the deity is in the one concept and how stiff and lifeless in the other. . . . Notice, too, how defective both concepts are; . . . *neither corresponds to its object.*" [29] Indeed, both personal and nonpersonal language are required for an adequate conceptualizing of God, and each acts as a valuable corrective on the other, but—and this is important—without religion as a living awareness, neither kind is of any value.[30]

Schleiermacher, in the notes to the third edition of the *Speeches,* vigorously defended himself against the charge of preferring the impersonal way of speaking. Yet the problem persists beyond the *Speeches* and reappears in *The Christian Faith.* The following comments may help to put the issue in perspective: First, Schleiermacher's discomfort with either a naïve theism or an empty and abstract monism is an expression of his profoundly Christian orientation. The ancient tension in Christian thought between divine transcendence and immanence is—as Schleiermacher rightly saw—rooted in the Christian consciousness of God. If God is to be religiously meaningful he must be sufficiently free from the chaos in which we live to be sovereign and, at the same time, sufficiently concrete and accessible to be the "living God," giving himself in the midst of that chaos. Naïve theism, like polytheism, submerges God in the order of time and reciprocity, and deprives him of his power over everything (Pannenberg). Its opposite deprives him of his concrete character as the giver and receiver of love.

Schleiermacher does not provide in the *Speeches* a formulation able to preserve both Christian insights equally. He continues to attempt, nevertheless, to hold together the transcendence and immanence of God—that is, to exempt God from the antitheses and tensions that characterize worldly existence in order that he might be the power of being and yet to preserve his character as the living God who gives himself in grace. Indeed, the most troublesome difficulties in the formulation of *The Christian Faith* concern the doctrine of God.

RELIGION AND THE RELIGIONS

The three concluding speeches pose fewer substantive difficulties and can be dealt with in a more summary fashion. Speeches three and four concern the societal character of religion. Since the factors that govern the generation of religions and also of communities within a given religion are similar, they can to a large extent be considered together. Schleiermacher is concerned to defend not merely religion but the concrete, historical realities called *religions*. He will not brook the assumption, all too common among his "cultured despisers," that religion *in abstracto* is desirable, but that its communal expressions are undesirable. A sustained polemic against the artificiality of Enlightenment rational religion reaches a climax in the third and fourth speeches. The emptiness of rational religion consists in the fact that it is no real religion at all, but an eclectic collection of dead fragments. It has not grown from a living intuition, but has been distilled from a dying form. It is attractive to many because, lacking any positive character, it offends no one.[31] It creates discussion groups but not churches; it rests on thoughts and not on feelings. It is no wonder that it appeals widely to the religiously indifferent, for it is an abstraction, and thus it stirs up none of the strong feelings aroused by concrete realities. Who can hate an abstraction? But then, who can love one?

True religion creates not abstract systems of thought but communities of faith. "Religion must be social if it is to exist at all."[32] This is true partly because men are social, but also because the genius of religion itself is social. Faith creates community because it drives the believer toward expression. He seeks those with whom he may share his wondrous vision, and also he looks to them for reinforcement. He desires hearers to whom he might confess his faith, and he also longs to become a hearer of those who bear witness to the same faith.[33] Therefore, no matter what the external accoutrements of dogma and organization, the essence of a religious confession is fellowship in which the awareness of faith is strengthened by mutuality. Thus the central activity of the church is worship, and the function of preaching is not to instruct but to evoke a sense of the mystery of God. Worship is testimony, proclamation, *kerygma*—activities in which the community returns to the source of its life.[34]

Ideally, the community of worship generates freedom. This is because it intuits the unity of all things in God and is not, therefore, threatened by difference. At least in its most mature expression it aims for the richest possible diversity of individual life within the wholeness of faith. Since it is human, it always falls short of the maturity to which it aspires, but this does not render the concrete religious fellowship unnecessary. The choice is never between a perfect church and a flawed one, but between an imperfect church which is a society of learners, sharing a life of worship, and a sterile individualism in which the spirit of religion languishes and dies.

Since the basic intuition of religion is always the same, whence arise differences? Why are there religions and not merely religion? The answer is that insofar as religion is always positive and historically conditioned, the way in which the religious feeling is expressed will vary accordingly. Each religion has its unique history and the forms it assumes reflect this special history. Thus is constituted the external side of religious particularity. It should not be assumed, however, that religion itself can be explained by reference to its historical origins. Such origins explain the differences between religions

but not religion *per se*, just as, one might say, the hills determine the contours of the road but do not account for the road's
coming to be in the first place. Only the power of the Infinite
acting upon us can explain the existence of religion. It is therefore a mistake to mark the historical limitation of a religion
and refuse to recognize the "higher causes" of which that historical community is an expression. Indeed, the rich variety of
religious expression is a desirable and healthy testimony to the
vitality of the divine in determining the various circumstances
of the world.

THE RELIGIONS AND THE CHRISTIAN RELIGION

The question of the relationship of religion in general to the
particular religions, and more especially to Christianity, dominates the final speech. Schleiermacher's concern with this issue
reflects the new awareness of world religions that accompanied
advances in comparative anthropology and the related social
sciences. His basic way of conceiving the relationship of Christianity to world religions once again sets the pattern for the
century that was to follow. He seeks to give a positive and
sympathetic account of the processes by which religions arise,
seeking those common elements that bind all worshiping communities together. At the same time he desires to defend the
uniqueness and superiority of the Christian faith.

There can be no real question of Schleiermacher's own
stance in relation to Christianity and the religions. He con-
fesses that, despite the methodological neutrality incumbent
on his defense of religious variety—that is, the attempt to
stand outside the particular community for purposes of analysis
and description—he cannot be wholly neutral regarding the
substance of Christian faith. He speaks as a believer for whom
the Christian faith is finally the ground upon which all that he
says must rest. Schleiermacher writes: "I cannot help being
concerned about whether you find the right vantage point from
which to view [religion]." [35] Yet this confession brings into

relief the methodological difficulty that permeates both the *Speeches* and *The Christian Faith*.

It is, of course, not so much Schleiermacher's problem as that of faith itself in a historical age. Religious confession arises from the particular community of faith, and to the extent that this is true, only those who stand within that community can grasp the inner logic of its faith. "Religion is only comprehensible," Schleiermacher reminds us, "through itself." [36] Thus as a sympathetic observer, he can scorn that kind of special pleading that sees other religions as fragmentary and preliminary to one's own. It is evident to him that, for its adherents, each religion has in itself its own eternal necessity.[37] Yet it is no surprise that his own examination of the history of religions reveals an upward progression at the pinnacle of which stands Christianity, the highest and holiest of all. Thus there appears within the *Speeches* a tension between the stance of the scientific phenomenologist of religion and that of the believing advocate, a tension that casts doubt on the descriptive analysis occupying the major portion of the final speech. It is precisely this tension that led crisis theology to abandon, at least in theory, the task of constructing a philosophy of religion and to adopt a frankly confessional stance.

What then, is the relationship of religion to the religions? Schleiermacher contends that there is no "religion in general," except in the sense that the awareness at its heart is everywhere the same. Religion becomes real and is manifest only in its historical forms. The origin of religious difference lies partly in the concrete historical situation, partly in the creative power of the revelation. Every religion, arising as it does from a unique history, reflects the positive qualities of its origins. But the particularity of religion is not merely inevitable, it is necessary and good. Schleiermacher commends to his readers not merely religion but *concrete* religion—the "all-too human" religions which are the object of so much Enlightenment scorn. For all their historical and human imperfections, they are alive; they show evidence of that inner glow which is the essence of religion and which is so signally absent in the abstractions his hearers praise. Natural religion is nowhere natural; it corresponds to no reality.[38]

Structurally understood, a religion is determined by its special way of viewing the universe—by its particular insight or intuition. This special insight then becomes the organizing principle for the integration of every other element of experience and gives the particular religion its characteristic quality. Since a religion seeks to interpret the whole world in the light of its fundamental insight, and since the source of that insight is the God upon whom all created things depend, religion properly excludes nothing; it is by nature inclusive. Particular religions therefore "select some one of the greatest relations of mankind in the world to the Highest Being and . . . make it the centre and refer to it all the others." [39] Each religion views the universe from its own unique perspective and therefore contributes to the manifold richness of the world of faith. Only when the central intuition of a religion is so narrowly delineated that other insights are excluded or lost does religion degenerate into sectarianism and heresy. Thus the measure of a healthy religion is the degree to which it integrates its various elements into a creative whole in which each is illuminated and enhanced by its governing intuition. Here, indeed, seems to be the germ of the concept of "fruitfulness" as a criterion of an adequate theology that Schleiermacher sets forth in *The Christian Faith*.[40]

By virtue of its unique and positive character on the one hand and its rootedness in the one divine reality on the other, every religion has a distinctive spirit and a common substance. Therefore the relation of the Christian faith to other religions is one of continuity. Christian faith seeks to discover the common piety that binds it to other communities of faith. It recognizes the struggle of the infinite to make itself manifest in all of the religions, yet it must finally assert that the union of the World-Spirit and the human spirit is revealed most fully in Christ. Just as the animism and polytheism of the ancients have in them the impetus toward monotheism, so even those religions that have achieved a higher level of universal wholeness reach toward fullest expression in Christ.

THE FORESHADOWING OF A MATURE THEOLOGY

The original perspective of Christianity is more glorious, more sublime, more worthy of mature humanity; it penetrates deeper into the Spirit of systematic religion and extends its scope more broadly over the entire universe. Purely and simply, it is the perception of the universal striving of all that is finite against the unity of the whole and of the way the deity deals with this resistance: of the way the deity reconciles this enmity.[41]

Schleiermacher's treatment of the Christian religion in the *Speeches* is extremely brief—a mere fifteen pages in Tice's translation. Yet it foreshadows key elements of his mature theology at more than one point and gives rise as well to serious problems with which he must wrestle subsequently. In the light of the foregoing analysis, he asks about the organizing intuition in the Christian faith, that insight which shapes all its other teachings and gives them their distinctive Christian character. In answering, he establishes the fundamental formula that provides the parameters for Christian theology in the third part of *The Christian Faith.* The insight that most adequately expresses the Christian perspective and that guides and integrates all other elements of its confession is the recognition of a polar tension between the world and God. The substance of all Christian theology is to be found in the resistance of all things finite to God and in the divine reconciliation by which it is overcome. "Corruption and redemption, alienation and reconciliation: These are two inseparably united and fundamental relations that constitute this mode of experience. The entire form and content of the religious matter in Christianity is determined by these dual relationships." [42] Thus according to Schleiermacher the central theological theme for Christian faith is sin and redemption; not that other religions lack these ideas, but in none are they so central or so determinative.

This definition of Christianity as the religion of sin and redemption requires brief comment, since it provides the basic paradigm for *The Christian Faith* and therefore determines the structure of Schleiermacher's mature, specifically Christian theology. As will be seen in his mature work, the general propositions of religion may be unfolded from the "feeling of absolute dependence," but the distinctly *Christian* theological affirmations arise from the experience of redemption from sin through Jesus Christ.

In describing the genius of Christian faith in terms of sin and redemption, Schleiermacher is, of course, taking his stance in the mainstream of Western theological tradition, at least since Augustine. In contrast to much Eastern Christianity, in which the motif of death and resurrection has been more prominent, Western Christianity has been more powerfully oriented toward the sin problem and has found its classic symbol in the cross. Although Schleiermacher has long since rejected the crude "blood" atonement of his Moravian background, his grasp of the Christian faith still finds its surest purchase in the sin-forgiveness motif to which his Moravian soteriology had spoken.

The vigor of Schleiermacher's description of the human dilemma—not only in the degree of its seriousness but in its permanence and unconquerability—is bound to surprise those who have too glibly charged liberalism, and through it Schleiermacher, with a superficial doctrine of sin. Schleiermacher, as early as the *Speeches*, takes his stand against all forms of simplistic humanism. If his descendants fell victim to a shallow humanism it is because they failed to listen to him with sufficient care. What is strongly implied in the last of the *Speeches* is made explicit in *The Christian Faith*, namely, that the tragic split in the human situation will persist for all foreseeable futures. It is the fundamental intuition of Christian faith that hostility to God is endemic to man. Every revelation of truth falters upon the obstinacy of the earthly sense. "Everything is torn away by the irreligious principle working deep within." [43] Furthermore, sin is born not merely of a corrupting environment, so that by the reforming of that environment men might rise above it. A corrupt environment indeed plays a part in the shaping of the specific sins of a generation or a nation, but it is not the source of sin. Sin arises from the rebelliousness of the heart.

This judgment is profoundly revealing with regard to Schleiermacher's fundamental anthropological stance and, since anthropology determines soteriology, with regard to the broader shape of his theology. In terms of the classic debate between anthropological rationalism and volitionalism, Schleiermacher stands with Augustine rather than with Thomas. Schleiermacher is a volitionalist, and this alone makes clear the gulf that separates him from the Enlightenment and explains his passionate rejection of the social optimism engendered by the rationalist confidence in men. Reason cannot alter the will, but can only serve it. "All evil . . . is a consequence of the self-seeking effort of the individualized nature, of its will to sever all connection with the whole, so as to be something entirely on its own. . . . Man's intellect is darkened, . . . his heart is corrupt, deficient in the praise of God." [44]

Once the reader takes seriously the hostility of the heart toward God, the sense of grace that dominates Schleiermacher's thought becomes eminently understandable. A strong doctrine of sin requires a strong doctrine of grace. Thus any suspicion that he harbors an implicit Pelagianism is firmly refuted. Self-salvation is ruled out. "When man does seek through self-consciousness to enter into fellowship with the unity of the Whole, the finite resists him, and he seeks and does not find and loses what he has found." And lest sin be excused as arising from the flesh only and not from the spirit, Schleiermacher makes his meaning clear. It is the waywardness of the *spirit* that makes the defective nature fatal to the sinner. "He wills rather than give heed. . . . In vain is every revelation."

However abundantly God reveals himself, "yet the ancient com-
plaint that man cannot comprehend what is of the Spirit of
God is never removed." [45] Sin requires grace; defective creation requires new creation.

It is the depth of its understanding of sin that elevates the
Christian religion, at least in principle, above "the religions,"
in that it provides its own principle of self-criticism, for it
directs its polemic not only against other religions but against
itself as well. [46] Christianity's "holy sadness"—that sense of un-
worthiness which underlies every Christian awareness—reflects
its understanding that even its own best piety stands in need of
reconciliation.

What is the place and significance of the Christ as reflected
in the *Speeches?* Schleiermacher's treatment of Christology is
brief in the extreme, yet it is clear that he has already come
much of the way toward the Christology of his systematic
period. What is crucial, he feels, in the founder of the faith is
neither the purity of his moral teachings nor the beauty of his
character, but "the great idea Jesus came to exhibit and the
marvelous clarity of that idea as realized in his soul," namely,
"that all finitude requires a higher mediation if it is to gain
union with the deity." [47] That is, conceptually considered, the
center of the Christ is again the word of sin and of redemption
that are from God. Christ makes clear the need of the human
heart for mediation and the reality of God's grace.

But Christ is for the believer not merely the one who reveals
the need for mediation and the availability of grace; he is
himself in some decisive manner the mediator of that grace.
Indeed, whatever the believer is able to say regarding Christ's
nature rests on the unequalled power with which he mediates
the divine favor. But if everything finite requires the mediation
of a higher being—if its union with the Whole has to be
awakened and sustained—then that which mediates must not
itself require mediation. If Christ appears to us as the one
who can mediate, and who therefore himself needs no mediation, then we must regard him as being more than finite. It is

the experience of the church not only that Christ did not share the finitude and sin that is our condition, and thus himself required no mediation, but that he possessed and communicated such an awareness of God that the church had no other way to conceive him except as himself belonging to the divine essence. "This consciousness of the singularity of both his knowledge of God and his being in God . . . was at the same time the consciousness of his office as mediator and of his divinity." [48]

As sketchy as the christological picture in the last speech remains, it shows clearly that a major shift in christological thought—one that provides the structure for the sweeping christological reconstruction of *The Christian Faith*—has already taken place. Henceforth for Schleiermacher, as for most subsequent Christian theologians, the traditional method of deriving Christology is reversed. In most past theology, including the reformed theology that provides much of Schleiermacher's heritage, the work of Christ as redeemer is dependent upon the nature of Christ as divine mediator. Thus in Calvin's *Institutes of the Christian Religion* the exposition of the two natures of Christ precedes and provides the necessary presupposition for the doctrine of reconciliation.[49]

While even in *The Christian Faith* this formal structure is retained and the doctrine of Christ's person considered before his work, nonetheless, for Schleiermacher all that can be meaningfully said about Christ's nature must be extrapolated from the reality of grace as experienced by the believer and the church. The direction is no longer from his person to his work (because of who he was, he could do what he did!) but from his work to his person. Because of what he has done for us—namely, mediated to us his unique awareness of and existence in God—we confess his participation in the divine essence. As in the *Speeches,* and even more in *The Christian Faith,* everything that can be said of Christ must relate to the experience of reconciliation through him which is the governing intuition of Christianity; and the "dignity" we attribute to the Redeemer "must be thought of in such a way that he is capable

of achieving this [reconciliation]." [50] Such a movement from
"work to person" is not only consistent with the experiential
method set forth in the *Speeches,* but reflects Schleiermacher's
awareness of the processes by which the church has moved historically from faith to confession.

Christ, then, for the Christian faith, is the decisive mediator
of God. But what of other faiths and other mediators? The
question of the uniqueness of Schleiermacher's Christ and the
finality of the revelation he mediates has been a persistent one.
Clearly his Christ has a certain finality for *faith,* but is it a
relative finality subject to being transcended by new and fuller
revelations? Might we not, at least in principle, look for others
to deepen and augment Jesus' revelation? It is also evident
that Christ has for the believer a certain uniqueness. No one
can be for us precisely what he is. But is this uniqueness historical only? Are others uniquely revelatory to those who stand
in other histories and live by other lights? Schleiermacher's
answer to this question is, from the standpoint of his mature
dogmatics, a highly unsatisfactory one, and seems to justify the
judgment of his critics that his Jesus is merely one of "many
Christs," each adequate and meaningful in his own place and
time but none final. And are not "many mediators" equivalent
to no mediator at all?

In the *Speeches* Schleiermacher concludes that Jesus never
claimed to be the sole mediator of God nor did he confuse his
school with his religion.[51] Similarly, despite his confessed
Christian advocacy, Schleiermacher seems unwilling to declare
the Christian faith qualitatively absolute. His caution is in part
methodological. The dual stance of the *Speeches* is evident in
these conclusions. Seen from the perspective of the phenomenologist, how can the adequacy of other mediators be denied?
Schleiermacher considers the possibility that Christian faith
may be transcended, at least in form, by more adequate faiths.
Indeed, part of the glory of Christianity is its humble recognition of its own relativity. This humility, coupled with Schleiermacher's sense of historical development, leads him to acknowl-

edge the temporal character of his own faith. Never does religion, even in its highest expression, escape its immersion in its own humanity.

This seems to be the final word of the speaker. It is, however, from the perspective of faith, a highly unsatisfactory word. Does not the questioning of the finality of Christ and his revelation of God cut the nerve of faith itself and mark the boundary between belief and unbelief? Whatever *forms* Christianity may later assume, must they not conform themselves to the ancient intuitions of that faith or else obliterate them? How far the author of *The Christian Faith* will go beyond the Christology of the *Speeches* is evident in the following meditation from the *Glaubenslehre.**

> It is possible to hope . . . that some day the human race, if only in its noblest and best, will pass beyond Christ and leave him behind. But this clearly marks the end of Christian faith, which on the contrary knows no other way to the pure conception of the ideal than an ever-deepening understanding of Christ.[52]

---

* The German term *Glaubenslehre* (lit., system of faith) has come into wide familiar use in Schleiermacher scholarship to mean Schleiermacher's theological system as set forth in *The Christian Faith*. It is also used throughout the present study.

III. The Christian Faith:
Religion, Theology, and God

The years between the publication of the *Speeches* (1799) and the first edition of *The Christian Faith* (1822–23) saw Schleiermacher moving ever more completely into the life of the university. The systematic and critical rigor manifest in *The Christian Faith* owes much to the demands of his academic career, but it is also the product of his immersion in Plato, who provided him with both incentive and model.[1] These years also saw an ever deeper involvement with the life of the church and a more profound awareness of historical Christianity. These were years in which Schleiermacher came to approximate in life and thought his own ideal of the thinking churchman in whom religious and scientific interests are conjoined in the highest degree.[2] It is in the ferment of these two interests—that of the honest, persistent scholar and the passionate believer—that *The Christian Faith* was born. It has been called, not without justification, the greatest systematic statement of Protestant theology since Calvin.

The contrast of style and tone between the *Speeches* and Schleiermacher's *Glaubenslehre* is immediately evident. Where the *Speeches* was rhetorical *The Christian Faith* is tightly reasoned, seeking for exactness of expression and comprehensiveness. The work is far more explicitly Christian in tone than the earlier work. Those who have seen in the author of the *Speeches* the scientific phenomenologist of religion are therefore hard pressed to understand the confessional character of the mature work. Some have even seen *The Christian Faith* as a work of descriptive scholarship by one who does not himself stand within the circle of faith. Such an error is possible only if one has failed to read the *Speeches* in the light of the Schleiermacher's life of service to the church. The Christian character of the *Glaubenslehre* results in part from its very different intent and audience. It is addressed not to the "cultured despisers" of the Berlin circle but to the Christian community. It is not a work of apologetics, but—as is all true theology— an exposition done on behalf of the church, expressing the convictions and intuitions by which that fellowship lives. No one who has taken seriously the descriptions of theology and of the theological task in the *Brief Outline* or shared the christological joy that radiates from the *Christmas Eve* can doubt that the author of *The Christian Faith* writes from within the "theological circle."

Yet the work is not blindly confessional; it is written with an eye toward making the meaning of Christian faith clear in the broader contexts of knowledge. In particular, Schleiermacher is concerned not only to say what is the essence of Christian truth but to make clear how that essence relates to the broader phenomenon of religion and to the growing body of truth in general. Thus while the concerns so central to the *Speeches* are still present, they are subordinated to the confessional task. Nevertheless, serious difficulties often arise from Schleiermacher's attempts to relate the concerns of the scientific scholar and the confessional theologian. The dual stance that gives the *Speeches* its sometimes problematic tone persists in new ways in *The Christian Faith,* foreshadowing the struggle of subsequent theology to speak for faith in ways that do not isolate the believer from the truths of a scientific and historical age.

The Christian Faith consists of two parts with a lengthy introduction and an important appendix. The introduction contains a historical and phenomenological examination of religion and of theology. Since such an examination is external and descriptive, its conclusions, according to Schleiermacher, are not theology proper but *prolegomena*. Nevertheless, this prolegomenon has important bearing on the subsequent dogmatics, for here his theological method emerges, as well as basic definitions that will have substantive significance for the theology proper.

Part one of the system contains propositions about God and the world derivable from the general religious experience described in the introduction as the feeling of absolute dependence, and shared by Christianity with other religions. It is this common ground, first delineated in the *Speeches*, that makes possible the Christian's kindred feeling with other worshipers everywhere. The feeling of absolute dependence, shared by all men, guarantees the universality of the divine self-revelation and ties all religious truth, wherever it may be manifest, to God. Thus part one of the system of dogma functions as a "natural theology," providing a general religious foundation on which a Christian theology can be erected. Part two of the system consists of the distinctly Christian doctrines that arise from the consciousness of redemption through Jesus Christ. The present chapter will examine the introduction of the dogmatics and part one. Chapter 4 will examine the explicitly Christian theology as it is developed in the second part of the system.

It is important to note at the outset that the distinctively Christian doctrines are not to be derived from the general religious consciousness. It is still common to hear the contention that for Schleiermacher all theology is derived from the feeling of absolute dependence. On the contrary, only those doctrines Christianity shares with other religions by virtue of having the same God are so derived. Christian faith, so far as it is to be distinguished from "religion in general," is rooted in the unique and, for the Christian, final manifestation of God in Christ. The reality of redemption cannot be deduced from the general awareness of the infinite in the world; indeed, what can be known about God and the world from the general religious consciousness is immeasurably heightened by the perspective of grace in which the believer stands. Part two of the system makes this clear. Nevertheless, the relationship of the two parts to each other will be a persistent question for the reader of *The Christian Faith*.

THE NATURE OF RELIGION

Dogmatics in the true sense arises from within faith. Any general description of religion, theology, or God, insofar as it relates to Christian dogma, can therefore only be preliminary, and of use in the Christian church only insofar as it is consonant with the faith of the church. But the language and categories by which we describe our faith arise from the social matrix of the church. Therefore, Schleiermacher proposes a preliminary examination of religion, theology, and God, employing "propositions borrowed from ethics." [3] By ethics, Schleiermacher does not mean moral philosophy in the narrow sense, but the science of the "ethos"—in modern parlance, philosophy of history or phenomenology of culture. The content of the Christian faith cannot be faithfully set forth until the meaning of the terms by which it is to be described is determined by reference to their origin and function in their ethos. Even theological language, to be intelligible, must be firmly rooted in the society of man.

What then is religion? The answer to this question in the *Glaubenslehre* is very similar to that given in the *Speeches*. What is new is the clarity of Schleiermacher's conception and a deeper grasp of the implications of his view. Finite being, he suggests, is characterized by an unending flux, a tension between disparate and often conflicting forces—by what Schleiermacher refers to as the "realm of antithesis." One experiences life in the world as an alternate abiding-in-self (*Insichbleiben*) and passing-beyond-self (*Aussichheraustreten*).[4] This is to say that we must define ourselves by reference to the world which "flows into" (in-fluences) us, but also we must define the world by reference to our own selves since we act upon and condition it. Abiding-in-self and passing-beyond-self Schleiermacher relates to the two forms of consciousness, knowing and doing.

Thus, for reasons set out in the *Speeches*, it will not do to identify religion either with abiding-in-self or with passing-beyond-self. Each of these forms of awareness is too much involved in the ebb and flow of particular existence to correspond to the reality of religion. But what of feeling, that third faculty of consciousness to which Schleiermacher had turned in the *Speeches?* Here his treatment reflects a new caution brought about, perhaps, by misunderstandings arising from his early employment of the term. If piety is to be related to feeling, care must be taken not to relegate religion to the realm of vague emotionalism bereft of intellective or practical significance. It must be carefully specified how religion as feeling is to be distinguished from the affective life in general. Not all feelings are "religious," nor is the man who feels most deeply the most pious. Particular emotions are aroused by particular events and actions and, as such, are as much in the flux, as ephemeral and insubstantial, as the events and objects by which they are occasioned. Religion can scarcely be identified with emotions as such.

Yet religion does have a special kinship to feeling, in that both seem to point to a primordial and invariable awareness that underlies the flux of experience. Emotional life has a kind of genetic priority. An infant has a pervasive life of feeling long before the other faculties emerge. Emotion also has a kind of structural or phenomenological priority. While the intellectual and volitional components of experience vary greatly from moment to moment, some affective tone is the invariable accompaniment of every state of willing or knowing. It is this felt continuity, this oneness of affective life, that points most clearly to the persistence of selfhood under the changing panoply of thought and action.[5] Insofar as religion is akin to feeling, it is so in reference to the deep and abiding awareness of personal unity under the flux of experience. Schleiermacher can call it therefore "immediate self-consciousness." [6]

The deepest datum of immediate self-consciousness is *givenness*. The fact that we are who we are is in part determined by our free decisions, but the fact that we are *at all* is the mystery to be comprehended. We are not the ground of our own being. Existence comes to us as a gift, and we neither create it nor do we sustain it. It is the deepest and purest expression of religion to affirm that if God "takes our breath away, we vanish into dust."

The primary datum of religion, then, has to do with dependence. But is every feeling of dependence religious, so that Hegel's dog, by virtue of his superior dependence, becomes a model of piety? Schleiermacher means nothing of the sort. In all normal relations, he suggests, we experience a mixture of dependence and freedom by virtue of the relativity of all things. We stand in a relation of reciprocity to everything; we are both conditioning and conditioned. This reciprocity of freedom and dependence applies even to the universe as a whole. The degree of the world's dependence on us as individuals is very small, but it is real. With our every step forward, the earth moves ever so slightly backward. We can have no feeling of absolute freedom or of absolute dependence with reference to anything, even the cosmos. This is why awe for the universe must never be mistaken for religion.

But at the heart of our experience is the total givenness of our being. Neither we nor the world have our "principle of existence" in ourselves. Big finitude and little finitude both point beyond themselves. To know that we depend on something that is not dependent on us—this is true piety. The source of all religion is therefore the "consciousness of being absolutely dependent, or which is the same thing, of being in relation to God." [7] The famed "feeling of absolute dependence" thus emerges as the logical consequence of Schleiermacher's attempt to delineate the religious intuition in a way that would distinguish it fundamentally from every other intuition. Moreover, this definition has important consequences for the further development of his theology. Several explanatory comments are in order:

1. To have this experience is to be in relation to God. Schleiermacher is confident that the feeling of absolute dependence constitutes an effective argument for God's reality. Indeed, he intends that it render unnecessary the usual proofs for the existence of God as they have been elaborated in the tradition of natural theology,[8] and especially as they have formed the core of much rationalistic-Enlightenment religion. Insofar as this is a proof of God it has an Anselmian flavor. Schleiermacher is critical of the ontological argument because it purports to move from concept to reality,[9] rather than from reality to concept, which is the proper direction. Yet the substance of Anselm's proof and of Schleiermacher's are much the same, and they both rest on a common epistemological basis. Anselm and Schleiermacher are both Platonists at heart and thus philosophical realists. This fact alone renders them incoherent to many of their nominalist critics. Both men assume there must be agreement between the fundamental ways in which we experience our world and the reality behind the world, or experience is falsified and coherence lost. For Anselm what we can *think* and what *is* must coincide or all knowledge becomes absurdity. This is why to the nominalist he seems to move from thought to reality in a surreptitious way. Similarly, Schleiermacher's conclusion that the feeling of absolute dependence is the same thing as being in relation with God seems akin to producing a rabbit out of a hat. It must be insisted that Schleiermacher is not making a Kantian gesture at this point. He does not mean that one has the feeling of absolute de-

pendence and can on the basis of it, if he likes, *postulate* God's existence. The conclusion is not optional; it cannot be denied without the most profound religious consequences. If you confess to a sense of absolute givenness and then deny that it corresponds to reality, the experience itself tends to collapse, and life, deprived of its ground, disintegrates. If so basic an intuition has no *fundamentum in re*, then the intuition is a lie and life loses its center.[10]

2. The feeling of absolute dependence is unitary and non-temporal (or, better, transtemporal) but it always comes to consciousness in a concrete situation of space and time. Therefore it will always be manifest in a variety of forms and expressions.

3. Since our felt relation to the universe is one of both freedom and dependence, the universe can never be the referent of the feeling of absolute dependence and therefore the object of worship. Thus pantheism is excluded. Despite its awesome majesty, the universe itself is dependent on that reality which is the ground of its being.[11]

4. Religion unites all of life without diminishing its richness. It moves to overcome the conflict and disharmony that characterizes life in the world but not in such a way as to deny the reality and value of historical existence. This error has sometimes made religion the ground for an unwholesome hatred of the world. Schleiermacher describes three grades or levels of consciousness. An animal, or perhaps an infant, has a kind of instinctual unity of feeling and action—of self and world. This unity is lost with the emergence of true self-awareness and consequent awareness of other selves and of the world. At this level life is characterized by infinite richness and complexity, but also by tension and conflict. This is the realm of antithesis. Its richness and intensity are bought at the price of lost innocence, of conflict between self and world, intellect and will, freedom and dependence. It is no wonder that there are times when the self remembers with dim longing the peace of infancy and yearns to return to the womb, or that religion has

sometimes felt that harmony and oneness could be achieved only by denial of the world.

But insofar as the feeling of absolute dependence arises with and under the flux of concrete experience, it points not backward to the womb but forward to a new and higher synthesis. True religion overcomes fragmentation, making us aware of the deep unity of life without destroying or obscuring the multiplicity and richness of existence at the second level. Thus Schleiermacher cannot be accused of advocating a mystical unity that swallows up the world. His is more nearly a "worldly Christianity" in which God is the "ground bass" (Bonhoeffer), unifying and giving depth to the whole. Maximum intensity of experience combined with maximum harmony—this is the goal of religion.

5. Religion creates community. Since the feeling of absolute dependence is an intuition of the unity of all being in God, it awakens in the worshiper a consciousness of kind and a feeling of oneness with all other creatures. This results in a sense of kinship with others and draws men together in community of worship. As Schleiermacher puts it in the *Speeches*, religious sensitivity drives toward association. Furthermore, since the pious awareness is awakened by concrete situations and is called forth by the contagion of witness, it will give rise always to specific and positive communities of faith—that is, churches. Positive religions are the necessary and desirable consequence of the feeling of absolute dependence.

6. The logical corollary of our absolute dependence is God's absolute independence. If God is the referent of the feeling of absolute dependence, then his freedom from the world and from causative influence must be complete, else the feeling toward him would be a mixture of dependence and freedom contradicting the pious intuition. Now, the reader should take note of this logical conversion because it is to have important consequences for the remainder of Schleiermacher's theological system and will generate serious problems for his attempt to develop a genuinely confessional Christian theology. Does God's absolute independence—his *aseity* in traditional terms—

render inconceivable all interaction or relation between him and his creation such as seems so crucial to the common language of Christian worship? The problem is not, to be sure, Schleiermacher's alone. It has haunted Christian thought through its history and has been especially evident since the synthesis of Aristotle and biblical theism in the Middle Ages. But it remains to be seen if the implications of the feeling of absolute dependence render impossible a solution to the dilemma upon which to so great an extent the theological enterprise in the last two centuries has foundered.

A question that will have an important bearing on the ones raised above must be asked at this point. Does the feeling of absolute dependence have cognitive content? Insofar as it is logically (and ontologically) prior to the sphere of "knowing," for Schleiermacher it appears to be precognitive, because to attribute to it an idea content would be to place it in the sphere of antithesis where all intellection takes place. Thus it would be subject to scientific criticism. If religion is not to be identified with dogmatics or theology it must not be confused with its idea content. Schleiermacher wishes to say that the root of piety is the timeless unity of intuition and feeling before their separation into the antitheses of thought and action. It cannot itself be conceptual and has no propositional character.[12] But if there is no determinant content, what provides the substance of theology? What one can say as a consequence of experiencing the feeling of absolute dependence is, as will be seen, by no means a matter of indifference. Indeed, the power of the feeling of absolute dependence to determine and regulate talk about God will be disturbingly evident in Schleiermacher's development of the doctrine of God.

The problem with which Schleiermacher is wrestling at this point is one that haunts all contemporary theology. The awareness of the finitude and cultural particularity of language, intensified by the fact of historical relativism, lies behind the development in the nineteenth century of the concept of religious symbol or myth. Schleiermacher, and David Strauss after him, sought a way to account for the tendency of all

language to disintegrate into absurdity when it refers to ultimate reality. To speak of God mythically or symbolically is to
do so in terms of time and space, and this means in the language
of the realm of antithesis which God, by his very nature,
transcends. Every attempt to formulate a "nonobjective theism,"
whether that of Barth, Tillich, or Buri, faces the problem
Schleiermacher here confronts: If the primordial religious
awareness is precognitive, how can it provide the raw material
for positive theology? If all statements about God are sym-
bolic—even the "feeling of absolute dependence" or "being
itself"—how do we choose between symbols? And we all do
choose! But if we admit to cognitive content in the religious
intuition, how do we exempt it from scientific and linguistic
criticism?

One thing seems certain: the feeling of absolute dependence
shapes its own intellective response. Niebuhr is certainly right
that the feeling of absolute dependence is not an empty sensa-
tion. To be aware of absolute dependence is to be aware of
reality. Neither must "feeling," as an aspect of selfhood, be
thought of as irrational, but as a dimension of the larger life
of reason the self constitutes. Niebuhr writes: "Feeling defi-
nitely has a cognizing function, although it can never pass over
into communication, as does the cognition that expresses itself
in language." [13] Schleiermacher is not proposing a nonobjective
theism, if by this one means the denial of all objective reference in religious feeling. To feel absolutely dependent is to *be*
in relation to God. Whatever the problems raised for his later
formulation, religion, for Schleiermacher, speaks not only of
the self but of God. Schleiermacher is, despite his misgivings
about all attempts to characterize the divine, a Platonist and
not Neoplatonist.

THE ESSENCE OF CHRISTIANITY

Since all religions share the feeling of absolute dependence
none is worthless. Christianity may be subsumed under the

general category of religion. How then can it be distinguished
and its relation to other particular religions understood? To
answer this question Schleiermacher undertakes a classifica-
tion of religions based on "propositions borrowed from
philosophy of religion." The details of this analysis need not
detain us here. The scheme he sets out is rather arbitrary and
now thoroughly dated. It does serve to remind us of the dawn-
ing awareness of the problem of cultural and religious plural-
ism and represents an early attempt to come to terms with it.
There has been, he suggests, a discernible upward movement
from primitive animism to monotheism. Indeed, Schleiermacher believes that no other direction has been possible.
Monotheism is destined to triumph: where or when has a people ever relapsed to animism, or even to polytheism, once it
arrived at a monotheistic faith? [14] Christianity is morphologically a species of monotheism, but it can be argued that it is
the highest type yet achieved because of its universalism (compare Israel and Islam) and its ethical depth and concern
(compare Islam and Eastern religions). As in the *Speeches,*
Schleiermacher seeks to set forth descriptively the unique intuition which is the organizing insight of the Christian religion: "Christianity is a monotheistic faith, . . . and is
essentially distinguished from other such faiths by the fact that
in it everything is related to redemption accomplished by
Jesus of Nazareth." [15]

The essential elements of this description are the same as
those set forth in the final speech. Redemption implies sin; it
points back to the tragic resistance of all things finite to God.
This sense of sin and longing for deliverance distinguishes the
Christian religion from those which consider man not to require
redemption (namely all forms of Pelagianism, Christian or
otherwise) as well as from those which, after the manner of
ancient Manichaeism, consider no healing of man or the cosmos
possible. For the Christian, redemption from sin by Jesus forms
the definitive experiential and doctrinal nexus—not that other
religions have no concept of sin and redemption, but in none

is this "transition" so central and determinative. Furthermore, while other religions have their founders or saviors, none, it would appear, relate redemption to their savior as does the Christian faith. He is not merely founder, teacher, or even revealer of the divine, but is himself uniquely redeemer. Other religions confess that the revelation can be conceived apart from the revealer. Christianity affirms that the revelation and the revealer are one.

Schleiermacher thus clarifies and extends the basic description of faith set forth in the *Speeches*, but this definition also contains a decisive step forward. All suggestion that Christian faith might hope to move beyond Christ has now vanished. One who is himself the *accomplisher* of redemption and who is himself endowed with redeeming power by God—this one remains at the center of faith. Schleiermacher makes it clear now that to seek to go beyond him would be to pass beyond the limits of Christian faith.[16]

THE NATURE AND FUNCTION OF DOCTRINE

It may be that the greatest significance of Schleiermacher for modern theology lies less in the substance of his thought than in the revolution he brought about regarding the nature and method of theology. Certainly, it is hard to see how nineteenth- and twentieth-century theology could have happened except on the basis of his methodological reformation. Of his recent critics, perhaps Barth alone has fully appreciated his impact in this area, but the understanding of the nature and function of theology in Barth's work is thoroughly Schleiermachian. Schleiermacher's search for a new theological method was prompted, on the one hand, by his grasp of the crisis created by the historical consciousness. In the future all men would recognize the historical and relative character of all dogmatic propositions, including those of the creeds and of the Scriptures themselves.

The fact was that no one henceforth could take the language

of theology to be timeless truths handed down by God. How could the church accept the particularity of its confessions and still argue for their importance and their relevance to the life of faith? Schleiermacher was motivated by a desire to rescue the church from the acids of relativism and to provide it with the tools by which it might be given new confidence and new capacity to reshape itself and its world. Schleiermacher was always the practical churchman, and theology, as he conceived it, had to be a living and growing thing if it was to serve the needs of a living church.

What then is doctrine or theology? "Christian doctrines are accounts of the Christian religious affections set forth in speech." [17] Religion is not knowledge, but it gives rise to knowledge or, more precisely, to expression. The deepest exaltation of the soul, if it is to be communicated, must be robed with the imagery and language of men, and such language always loses something of the immediacy of the ecstasy from which it springs. Religious language, therefore, arises from faith and has no meaning unless it points back to the religious intuitions it seeks to express. Theology is not faith, it is the rational *expression* of faith.

By distinguishing theology from religion, or the language of faith from faith itself, Schleiermacher opens up the way to a complete rethinking of Christian doctrine. He is nowhere the father of modern theology more characteristically than in fixing this principle for all time. It is henceforth possible to distinguish the reality of faith from the formulation by which the believer or the church gives expression to it. This insight had taken shape for Schleiermacher in the Dohna household at Schlobitten. There he had discovered that a bond of faith could exist between those whose dogmatic expression differed greatly. There he had learned to seek beyond appearance for "the inner nature of things."

The distinction between religion and theology as religion's doctrinal expression had profound and liberating implications for the church. First, it allowed a frank recognition of the his-

torical character of dogma. That is, the church could on
Schleiermacher's terms admit the finitude of doctrinal formulations as products of time and space without surrendering the
timeless reality they express. Furthermore, it freed the church
and the theologian from the impossible task of defending all
past dogma as eternal truth. Only by escaping the rigid
creedalism and biblicism that confused the faith of the church
with its past expressions could the task of reshaping dogma for
a new age begin. Finally, it made possible a new graciousness
among theologians and believers, since it was no longer necessary to assume that differences in theology meant differences in
faith. It is not too much to say that ecumenical Christianity as
it is known in the present day would have been impossible
apart from the redefinition of doctrine set out in the *Glaubenslehre.*

THEOLOGY AND THE RELIGIOUS AFFECTIONS

If doctrine is the explication of religious experience, then
it follows that no dogma is legitimate unless it can be referred
back to some aspect of the religious affections. This dictum,
when taken seriously, has a clear usefulness to the church in the
evangelistic task, since it can appeal directly to the experience
of the hearer. It also has an immediate and perhaps salutory
winnowing effect on the body of doctrine, since any dogma
which makes no contact with the religious intuition is seen to
be of questionable value. Schleiermacher's suspicion of empty
speculation in theology grows out of his conviction that theology must keep its roots deep in the soil of faith. Now,
Schleiermacher's own feeling for the historical church served as
a restraint on the too-easy elimination of the elements of tradition
and led him to seek with uncommon persistence the intuitions of
faith underlying many an abstruse dogma. His disciples were
sometimes less cautious, and at times the task of pruning the
theological vine was done with far too little discretion. The
narrowing and simplifying of doctrine associated with some

forms of liberalism suggests the danger of such an experiential criterion when applied with a deficient sense of history.

The experiential criterion described above and the questionable use made of it by subsequent theologians bring to the fore the charge of subjectivism frequently leveled at Schleiermacher. Does the demand that all theology be validated by the religious consciousness represent a removal of all objective criteria and make man the measure of all the truth? While an issue of such long standing cannot be resolved here, the following observations may be helpful:

1. Schleiermacher is a subjectivist in the sense that according to him we meet God first and foremost in our deep "inwardness." There is no objective fact, whether God or the world, that is not mediated through experience. This truism, implicit in all Western thought since Descartes, became explicit with Kant. Schleiermacher's virtue is the clarity with which he saw this fact and the candor with which he acknowledged it. Nor have Schleiermacher's objectivist critics succeeded in evading the "subjectivist principle," as is witnessed by the appeal of crisis theology to "existential verification" or to "truth as encounter" (Brunner).

2. Schleiermacher is not a subjectivist in the sense that God can be whatever the believer wants him to be. The experience on which dogma rests is not self-generated; its distinguishing mark is its *givenness*. In making religious statements one is not merely describing his feelings and making no comment on the reality beyond. As has been seen, the feeling of absolute dependence is its own refutation of subjectivism. Schleiermacher's realism is at work here. You cannot have the feeling of absolute dependence and then deny its objective reference. To do so would destroy the feeling. It is precisely the religious intuition that drives beyond subjectivism. If the awareness of God does not lift us above solipsism, nothing can.

3. The question may persist whether the reference of theology to feeling makes every person his own criterion and results in a lonely individualism—"God and the soul, the soul

and its God" (Harnack). This was certainly not Schleiermacher's intention, since religion is by nature social and
theology is the work of the community. Thus the subjectivity
of the individual Christian is limited by the subjectivity of the
church, both present and past. The theologian's task is to find
an ever more adequate expression not merely for his own faith,
but for that of the fellowship he serves.

THE CRITERIA FOR AN ADEQUATE THEOLOGY

But how do you judge an adequate theology? On the basis of
its nature and function, a theology must be judged in two ways:
by reference to its object and by reference to its purpose. The
object of Christian theology is "the Christian religious affections"; its purpose is to set these affections forth in coherent
speech. Schleiermacher enumerates the formal criteria for
theology: "Dogmatic propositions have a twofold value—an
ecclesiastical and a scientific; and their degree of perfection is
determined by both of these and their relation to each other." [18]

The *ecclesiastical* value of a doctrine has to do with its faithfulness to the religious affections of the community from which
it springs. Theology is confessional and must be tested to make
certain that it is true to the faith of the church. If it fails in this
test all subsequent tests are meaningless, for it then becomes,
in the words of the *Speeches*, an attenuated religion with no
"middle point" and thus no concrete substance.[19] To put it
another way, doctrine must elicit recognition. It must stir the
believer or the church to respond, "Yes, that is right! That is
what I have felt and know to be true."

But its adequacy must also be measured by its *scientific
value*. By this Schleiermacher means its intelligibility and internal coherence. Theology is not excused by its confessional
character from the necessity of intellectual honesty and integrity. Once it chooses to employ language, it is bound by the
rules of thought and logic that make communication possible.
Theology must not only express faith, it must make sense. Now,
Schleiermacher understands that there are different levels of

expression and that not all require the same logic. He distinguishes three types of religious speech—the poetic, rhetorical, and descriptively didactic—each arising from a different need or function of the church. The first two, manifest primarily in liturgy and preaching, are of doctrinal significance, but since their aim is not scientific, they are allowed an indefiniteness of expression not permitted theology in the purest sense. True dogmatic propositions are "doctrines of the descriptively didactic type, in which the highest possible degree of definiteness is aimed at." [20] By the nature of the theologian's task, he is not allowed the inconsistency or imprecision permitted to poetry, devotional literature, or even preaching.

The scientific value of a doctrine can also be expressed as its *fruitfulness*—that is, its many-sidedness. A sound theology might begin its exposition at almost any point, but one would then be led to consider and better comprehend every other dimension of faith. For example, a doctrine of God that renders human freedom incoherent is less fruitful than one that leads to a fuller appreciation of freedom, sin, and grace. In summary, two questions must be asked of any doctrine which is presented to faith: (1) Does it make sense, both internally and with reference to truth in general? (2) Is it true to the faith from which it springs?

Two final comments are in order concerning the character of theology:

1. *Theology is the church's tool of self-criticism.* Although nothing is further from Schleiermacher's intent than narrow heresy-hunting, he understands that if the church is to retain its unity, it must establish principles by which some propositions will be adopted and some excluded. Only by defining its central core with adequate clarity is it possible to establish the limits within which a true theology can be developed. Whatever transcends those limits and threatens the unity of the faith it seeks to express is heresy. It will be seen below how this methodological principle functions for Schleiermacher in setting the limits for Christian faith.

2. *Theology is temporal and changing.* If theology is the ex-

pression of the church's faith, and the church is a living, historical reality, undergoing new experiences with every generation, then it follows that theology also is a living thing. The changing character of language and of social understanding—these alone are sufficient to require that theology change in order to remain true to its timeless insights. Thus dogmatic systems set forth "the doctrine prevalent in the Christian Church at a given time." [21] That is to say, "system" must not be confused with "summa" (Tillich). Theology must ever remain open to the new or it will become rigid and die—and this means even the system of *The Christian Faith.*[22]

THE DOCTRINE OF GOD

The first part of the system proper aims at "the Development of that Religious Self Consciousness which is always both presupposed by and contained in every Christian Religious Affection." [23] Thus this part of Schleiermacher's dogmatic has a kind of systematic equivocacy or ambivalence, since it is both "pre-Christian" and Christian. Its purpose is to draw out the implications of the nature of God from the general God-consciousness shared by Christian and non-Christian alike. If this is done honestly, without influencing the explication by hidden Christian intuitions, Schleiermacher feels the result will be an understanding of the divine nature adequate to any thinking piety. What Christianity shares with other religions is God as the referent of the feeling of absolute dependence. The reality made evident in the God-consciousness, then, is "contained in every Christian religious self-consciousness." [24] Therefore the development of the general God-consciousness is intended to lay a foundation for a distinctly Christian theology that will rest not merely on the feeling of absolute dependence but on the consciousness of redemption through Christ.

Thus the overall structure of *The Christian Faith* consists of a kind of general theology supplemented and made complete by Christian dogma. Such a structure is reminiscent of many

other efforts to bring together the general religious consciousness and the demands of Christian dogmatics, for example,
that of Aquinas, or, in the evangelical tradition, some types of
Calvinist orthodoxy. By adopting this familiar procedure,
Schleiermacher seeks to accomplish what every such attempt at
synthesis has sought, namely, (1) to establish the universality
of divine self-manifestation and therefore protect the goodness
of God, (2) to unify the Christian understanding and establish
the continuity of all religious knowledge—that is, to establish
that all truth, whatever its immediate source, is ultimately
from God—and (3) to provide a "point of contact" for the
Christian mission in the universal awareness of the divine oc-
curring in all men.

However, the assumption of a common "religious a priori"
shared by Christian and non-Christian alike is risky, especially
if this means that the general God-consciousness shapes and
conditions what can be said from the perspective of Christian
faith. Schleiermacher seems to assume that the feeling of
absolute dependence underlies the Christian experience of
grace as a kind of prerequisite and that the general God-
consciousness and the Christian's "Christ-consciousness" are
in all respects mutually supportive and compatible. But these
assumptions require critical examination. Several questions
are in order:

1. How does the feeling of absolute dependence function in
conditioning or determining the doctrine of God? The question
was asked above whether the feeling of absolute dependence
has a cognitive content, or whether it functions merely as a
"limiting concept." If it is purely abstract or formal—an
analytic definition of "that which concerns us ultimately"—
then it might establish religion in general and the Christian
religion on the same ground without prejudicing the contents
of Christian dogmatics in any way. Does the feeling of absolute
dependence have "content"? In part one the answer seems to be
a qualified yes; or at least one must, in Niebuhr's terms, consider it a "cognizing function." But it is not so easy to say

with Niebuhr that it "can never pass over into communication,"[25] since the feeling of absolute dependence has for
Schleiermacher certain clear implications concerning what can
or cannot be said about God.

2. This being the case, how does the content of the general
God-consciousness relate to the specifically Christian consciousness? Do they always coincide? What if the feeling of
absolute dependence conflicts with what Christian experience
seeks to say about God? Which then is the norm? Which judges
the other? Put in another way, from what perspective does one
finally write theology, from that of the feeling of absolute dependence or that of the Christian self-consciousness? The
answer Schleiermacher clearly intends is from both, since he
operates on the assumption that they must always reinforce
one another. Thus a doctrine of God drawn from the general
God-consciousness can function as well for the Christian as for
the Moslem or the Hindu, and the equivocacy of this part of
the system is justified. In fact, however, the compatibility of
the two is far from self-evident, and one cannot escape the
feeling, at least in part one, that wherever tension arises between these perspectives the feeling of absolute dependence
prevails. Schleiermacher does not hesitate to reject or to demythologize traditional propositions about God on the grounds
that they would conflict with the feeling of absolute dependence.[26]

But can a Christian theology, and especially one so explicitly confessional as Schleiermacher seems to intend, put up
with such a dominance? The manner in which the feeling of
absolute dependence holds sway in part one generates deep
problems for the rest of his system. The difficulty is the one
that has troubled every attempt of Christian theology to recon-
cile the general awareness of the divine with the knowledge of
God in Christ. How does one relate the transcendent perfection
and metaphysical universality demanded of "being-itself," and
the concrete God of biblical revelation? How does one build a
bridge between "pure act" and perfect love? The problem is, of

course, not of Schleiermacher's making but has haunted Christian theism since its first confrontation with the philosophical tradition. From Plato and Aristotle, through Plotinus, Augustine, Aquinas, and even Calvin to Barth and Tillich, the tension between the absolute potency of God and the divine love are never fully resolved. It is no surprise that Schleiermacher confronts it also, but it will be equally surprising if a theologian of his perceptiveness can allow this difficulty to go unnoticed, for it clearly imperils the "fruitfulness" of his theology. Unless he can demonstrate the compatibility of the feeling of absolute dependence and the Christian awareness, these will become not twin foci of the same ellipse but conflicting centers of religious consciousness, and his theology, like many that have come before, will disintegrate into incoherence. On the basis of his doctrine of God, it is not difficult to understand why critics have discounted the "Christian" theology of part two as purely descriptive and concluded that Schleiermacher's true God, as required by the feeling of absolute dependence, is the abstract absolute of speculative idealism. It remains to be seen whether Schleiermacher can defend himself against the charge of creating a philosophy of identity.

The seriousness of the problem becomes immediately evident as he sets out the general doctrine of God. The method by which Schleiermacher "unfolds" the doctrine has been set forth in the introduction. All dogmatic propositions are first of all descriptions of the content of the pious self-consciousness, but insofar as the religious awareness points beyond itself to its "whence," they are also statements about God. Furthermore, insofar as this whence is felt to be the power of coherence in all things, religious statements are also about God in his relation to the world. Thus the doctrine of God is developed under three forms; it treats of (1) our experience of God, (2) the nature of God in and of himself, that is, "the attributes of God in relation to the world as they appear in that self-consciousness," and (3) God's relation to creation, or "the constitution of the world as therein conceived by virtue of its absolute de-

pendence on God." [27] As shall be seen, it is the nature of God
as creator, derived from the feeling of absolute dependence,
that decisively shapes what may be said of God in himself.

GOD AS THE CAUSE OF THE WORLD

We experience God primarily as creator. This, Schleiermacher feels, is implicit in our consciousness of ourselves and
of the world as dependent on him. But the doctrine of creation
is not an attempt at a cosmology, it is a religious confession.
To understand it as a cosmology—that is, as a description of
the origins of the physical universe—would be to put it on a
collision course with modern science. The doctrine of creation,
as a *religious* doctrine, speaks not of world origins but of the
fundamental relations that pertain between God and the world.
Strictly speaking, faith cannot talk about creation. We have
no experience of beginnings, but only of God's sustaining
activity in us and in the world. Yet the religious essence of the
doctrines of creation and of divine preservation (or conservation) are the same, namely, that all things receive their being
from and are absolutely dependent on God. Thus the two
propositions of creation and conservation coalesce into the religious affirmation that he is the power in all that is. The confession that God created "out of nothing" is understandable
and true only if it is a commentary on the dependence of all
things on him. It has nothing to do with the origin of physical
matter, but affirms that there is nothing "out there," over
against God, that does not bear the mark of his character. Thus
there is no "realm" that can finally frustrate his providential
activity. *Creatio ex nihilo*, then, is essentially a rejection of
dualism, and the concept of divine creation is an affirmation
about the quality of existence as it comes from God. Nothing
can be excluded from the divine causative activity or find in
itself its own power of being, not even the world. Several comments are in order at this point:

1. Note should be taken of Schleiermacher's method and of

the purpose he seeks to accomplish by it—at every point to get behind the limited, time-bound language of dogmatic and creedal formulations to the religious substance they contain; that is, to go behind what they say in order to discover what they are *saying*. This search for the real religious essence, Schleiermacher feels, is the only way the past confessions of faith can be made to meet the two criteria of theology, the confessional and scientific. He seeks to elicit recognition ("This is what we really feel and believe") without arousing a sense of absurdity. What can the idea of divine creation mean, given the "death of Adam"? It is not theology's task to resurrect Adam, but to discover the timeless, religious intuition the Hebrew account sought to express. The kinship of Schleiermacher's method to the existential methodologies of some twentieth-century theologians is evident here,[28] and his handling of creation clearly anticipates the practices of neoorthodox hermeneutics. The debt to Schleiermacher of Tillich and of Bultmann in particular is considerable.

2. Schleiermacher's deep sympathy for Christian tradition should be observed in his handling of the idea of creation. It is precisely his appreciation for the historic confessions that has led to his quest for "inner substance." Throughout *The Christian Faith* the reverence with which he examines the biblical and dogmatic statements for their experiential truth is evident. Even those elements of tradition that give him the greatest difficulty—for example, the dogma of the Trinity—are treated with the greatest earnestness and circumspection. True to his own ideal, he is seeking to be both an honest man and a responsible interpreter of the church's faith.

3. God is always experienced through the world, just as the pious self-consciousness always arises in and through the events of nature and history. This means that we need not rupture the "fabric of nature," as described by science, in order to get God into the world. God is not manifest in the absence of natural order but is the reality shining through the things and events of the world. This understanding opens the way to a

new concept of miracle, one that can coexist with an honest appreciation of natural science. This understanding was essentially complete as early as the *Speeches*. Since all of nature is capable of stirring up religious feeling, every finite thing is at least potentially a vehicle for the Infinite. To apprehend God in the ordinary—*this* is miracle. Thus Schleiermacher could say in the second speech, "Miracle is simply the religious name for event." [29] The miraculous element lies not in the character of the event but in the subjective appropriation of God manifest in and through it. He does not intend hereby to espouse a rigid mechanistic view of nature such as was appearing in Enlightenment physics; how far he is from intending a closed, causal system of nature which excludes creativity and novelty will become evident in the discussion of his Christology. Nevertheless, his definition of miracle as a religious and not a scientific category has become the guiding one in most contemporary Christian thought. [30]

It should also be noted that there appears to be little provision in Schleiermacher's thought for a direct "I-thou" encounter with God apart from the world. The kind of neo-Pietism encountered in later liberalism (Harnack, Herrmann), with its implicit individualism, is foreign to Schleiermacher. This is clearly the case regarding the doctrine of God, arising as it does from the feeling of absolute dependence, but it is scarcely less the case with reference to Christian doctrine. The believer's relation to Christ is real, but it can never be divorced from the concrete worshiping community, its liturgy, and its community of love. Insofar as Christ is encountered redemptively, it is within, not apart from, the life of the church.

Since the primary datum of religion is dependence (ours and the world's), we are aware of God primarily as "cause," since to be absolutely dependent is to be absolutely caused. Everything that exists does so by virtue of the creative activity of God. Thus divine creativity or causality becomes the determinative content of the doctrine of God. Schleiermacher immediately reminds the reader, however, that divine creativity must not be thought of in such a way as to resemble human activity, for this would involve God in the finite realm and deprive him of his character as the Infinite.

Now, the decision of Schleiermacher to identify God with causality and then to insist that divine causality differs fundamentally from finite causality raises so many difficulties for his subsequent doctrines that it threatens the coherency of his system. Why does he feel compelled to move in this direction? He is certainly motivated in part one by the fear of anthropomorphism expressed earlier in the *Speeches,* but this fear itself arises from the theological dilemma also referred to previously, namely, the paradox of the divine transcendence and immanence. Biblical faith finds it necessary to affirm a God sufficiently concrete and available to be the object of worship and yet at the same time sufficiently free of and above the chaotic forces of concrete reality to be able to order and redeem them. Tillich is correct: one cannot worship an abstraction; but is it not equally true that a God who is subject to the vicissitudes of the finite world is not worthy of worship?

Schleiermacher's use of causality as the determinative category for developing the doctrine of God is an application of the classic analogy of being,[31] with all of its accompanying strengths and weaknesses. Like the Enlightenment deist, he is moving from the mode of divine presence experienced in the world to the reality of God, but unlike the deist, he understands that the analogy of finite being falsifies as well as characterizes. Deistic gods always end up slaves to the world, limited by the world with which they work and therefore unworthy of worship. So, also, Schleiermacher feels, God would be a slave to the world if his causality is thought of as a part of the mutual interdependence of causes in the world. If he is not preeminent causality, then he is indistinguishable in principle from the world. The aseity of God is expressed religiously as the logical corollary of absolute dependence. By the principle of logical inversion, the absolute dependence of the creation requires the absolute independence of God.[32]

The consequences of this logical inversion are momentous. God cannot be thought of as involved in the reciprocity of the world, for then he would be conditioned as well as conditioning. Furthermore, since the order of finite causality is the order of time and therefore of change, God's creative activity must never be conceived as temporal activity, for thus "the antithesis between Him and finite beings would be lessened and the purity of the feeling of absolute dependence endangered." [33]

Thus Schleiermacher, like many traditional theists, seeks to protect the preeminence of God by qualifying decisively every categorization drawn from the language of time and space. Every analogy falsifies and must be stripped of its limiting character before it can apply to God. But by exempting God from the antitheses of the world, the problems that have haunted the theology of the past reappear. What finally can it mean to speak of God if he transcends all meaningful language? Does not all talk of God collapse into mystic silence? Schleiermacher understands the problem and wrestles with it valiantly. He wishes to affirm a God real enough to be the object of men's love, but the principle of divine independence makes his task a difficult one.

Again it appears that the feeling of absolute dependence is functioning as the decisive norm for what can be said about God. The way Schleiermacher deals with the divine attributes is instructive. The traditional attributes of God are to be understood "as denoting not something special in God, but only something special in the manner in which the feeling of absolute dependence is to be related to him." [34] Thus they refer to *nothing real* in God, but only in our way of relating to him or of experiencing him. Now, Schleiermacher does not mean that divine attributes are vacuous. Rather, they are time and space responses to God, that is, myths and symbols. Because the feeling of absolute dependence (and surely the Christian intuition as well) demands the essential oneness and indivisibility of God, whatever refers to God must refer to all of him. Every attribute therefore must describe in some way the whole of God in his creative activity, *but as seen from a different human perspective.* Omnipotence, omniscience, eternality—these are not different parts of God which compositely constitute his nature. They must rather be ways of describing the unified action of the one God, else we are threatened by a divine schizophrenia in which, for example, God's holiness is seen to be at war with his love.

Schleiermacher's intention becomes clear when we follow his application. All attributes finally are reducible to that of *omnipotence,* for this expresses the "Absolute Causality to which the feeling of absolute dependence points." [35] Therefore the *eternality* of God can best be comprehended as divine omnipotence considered from the perspective of time, so that to speak of God as eternal is to say that there is no conceivable time—past, present, or future—in which his omnicausality would not be manifest. Considered spatially, omnipotence is omnipresence. In a similar way he seeks to unify the attributes of God under the governance of the feeling of absolute dependence.

COMMENTS ON THE DOCTRINE OF GOD

What is to be said concerning Schleiermacher's theological procedure in part one and of the resultant doctrine of God? Insofar as he seeks to relate the doctrine of God faithfully to the feeling of absolute dependence, he meets the first test of theology, namely, the ecclesiastical, and the pious soul will recognize in it the God he worships. Also, insofar as the feeling of absolute dependence and the Christian self-consciousness reinforce one another, the Christian will also cry "Abba, Father!" Finally, by seeking to unify all disparate elements of traditional theologies under the one principle of divine causality, he seeks to meet the "scientific" criterion, and to satisfy the legitimate demands of speculative thought about God.

But can the theologian really serve three masters? If the demands of speculation, of religion in general and of Christian faith can be brought into perfect agreement, what a tour de force he will have achieved. If they cannot—if, after all, the requirements of the feeling of absolute dependence and of the Christian faith do not always reinforce one another—what then? The Christian theologian does indeed recognize himself in Schleiermacher's doctrine of God. He is likely to feel that Schleiermacher is wrestling with the concerns that have always occupied the thinking of the church, and that he is doing so with creativity and originality. His God is the omnipotent, omniscient, eternal, infinite creator and cause of all things. This suits well with the experience and the testimony of the community of Christian faith. Why, then, does the feeling of discomfort persist? Perhaps it is because by bringing into focus the power of the church's traditional "God-talk" he has also revealed with new clarity its problems for faith.

One might observe that Schleiermacher's doctrine of God is marked, in part one at least, by a rather Calvinist tendency. All the attributes boil down to omnipotence. And it could be argued that an adequate Christian doctrine of God requires more. Expressed "religiously," does it not require both divine sovereignty (or providential control) and love? Without either it becomes questionable whether God is "religiously available." The emphasis of Calvin and Schleiermacher on the omnipotence of God squares well with the feeling of absolute dependence; it also meets half of the needs of Christian faith. Therefore, it falls on receptive ears up to a point. But by itself, omnipotence tends to become *bare* omnipotence, and it generates profound difficulties for conceiving the divine love. It is instructive that the "personal attributes" of God receive very short shrift here. If, in the final analysis, the feeling of absolute dependence denies any concrete character to God save that he is bare cause, then the language of redemption, which determines part two of the system, can refer to "nothing real in God."

Here the nature of the chasm that threatens to split the system becomes clear: how can the absolute independence of God be squared with the requirements of redemption? Unless this chasm can be bridged, then *The Christian Faith* cannot pass Schleiermacher's own test of fruitfulness. No satisfactory answer is forthcoming in part one. Despite certain passages that suggest fruitful possibilities, one moves to the next part of the *Glaubenslehre* with misgivings. Any final evaluation of Schleiermacher's theological achievement must ask to what extent he is able to move beyond the chasm and unite the feeling of absolute dependence and the Christian consciousness into a coherent whole.

THE TRINITY

Schleiermacher's treatment of the doctrine of the Trinity in part one is extremely brief and of such a nature as to justify, at first glance, the charge of Unitarianism. He foregoes extensive treatment of the Trinity not only because the suggestion of distinctions in the divine threatens to involve God in the realm of antithesis but also because, as he sees it, "the doctrine of the Trinity is neither presupposed in every Christian religious experience nor contained in it." [36] However, this brief, almost flippant disclaimer does not represent Schleiermacher's last word on the subject. In the very last section of *The Christian Faith* he provides a more sensitive commentary, which shows far deeper appreciation of the ecclesiastical significance of the dogma. He rightly sees that the dogma has arisen from the Christian sense that the God who is manifest in the world has also made himself manifest redemptively in Christ and in the common spirit of the church. He has also grown increasingly aware of the pivotal importance of the doctrine for a meaningful explication of the Christian idea of redemption. Wherever the doctrine of the Trinity has been rejected, he admits, one finds always a breaking up of that central doctrinal core which determines, according to *The Christian Faith*, the substance of Christian dogma. Schleiermacher observes that the abandoning of the Trinity almost always results in a changed doctrine of man, Christ, and redemption. Therefore if the dogma is understood as a religious affirmation that divine creative and redemptive activity in all its dimensions is one, then it is quite truly the "coping-stone of Christian doctrine." [37] If the dogma is an attempt to set forth metaphysical divisions in the Godhead, then it is an exercise in fruitless speculation that violates both the demand of the feeling of absolute dependence and the Christian insistence that the wholeness of God be actively manifest in his every activity.

IV. The Christian Faith:
Sin and Redemption

The second part of *The Christian Faith* has not received the scholarly attention given to the first part. This may result from the difficulty of understanding how the Christian intuitions can be made coherent in the light of the demands of the feeling of absolute dependence. Thus many early interpreters concluded that the real heart of the work lay in the doctrine of God. However, failure to take seriously Schleiermacher's doctrine of sin and redemption is to distort his entire theology. His own deep involvement in the Christian faith and in the life of the church is revealed by the profound sensitivity with which he seeks to interpret that faith and life for his time. He is never more brilliant than in his rethinking and reshaping of the doctrines of the Christian community.

THE CRITERION OF CHRISTIAN DOCTRINE

Christian doctrine arises not merely from the general religious consciousness; it is generated above all by the consciousness of redemption from sin through Jesus Christ. This consciousness is the particular form in which the feeling of absolute dependence comes to expression in the positive religion of Christianity. Christian doctrines, then, are Christian intuitions set forth in speech, and every proposition purporting to be Christian must validate its claim by reference to Christian experience. Any truly Christian doctrine must be extrapolated from the awareness of redemption central in the Christian community. The purpose of the second part of the system of doctrine is to draw out the implications of that uniquely Christian experience.

What is the heart of the Christian intuition as Schleiermacher perceives it? The answer, set forth as early as the *Speeches*,[1] is reiterated in the Introduction of *The Christian Faith:* "Christianity . . . is essentially distinguished from all other faiths by the fact that in it everything is related to the redemption accomplished by Jesus of Nazareth."[2] Considered from without, this delineation is descriptive, serving to assign the Christian religion a historical position in the panoply of world religions: Christianity is that religion the center of which is redemption from sin accomplished by Jesus Christ. Considered from within, it is definitive: Whatever fails of interpretation by this central intuition cannot be considered essential to Christian faith. Whatever violates or renders the awareness of redemption ineffective must be rejected. Therefore the above definition provides the formal criterion for Christian dogma; furthermore it provides the governing structure for the second part of the system. Several important consequences follow for Christian doctrine:

1. Any adequate Christian theology will give expression to two governing motifs, namely, sin and redemption. Other religions include these motifs, but in none are they so dominant as to be definitive. You cannot have Christianity without both. Furthermore, in Christianity, redemption must be referred in all its aspect to Jesus not merely as a founder, for then the difference between Christian faith and other historically grounded faiths would be external only. In Christianity the relation of the founder to the members of the communion is

more than instrumental, it is determinative; he is not only founder, he is Redeemer; the transition from sin to redemption is not only made manifest but accomplished by him.[3]

2. The antithesis of sin and redemption sets the limits of Christian doctrine. Every theology seeks to express as exhaustively as possible the insights of its faith and to exclude all that would falsify or distort that faith. Schleiermacher concludes that, in order for an adequate and healthy theology to come to birth, "it is necessary first to eliminate from the total mass of dogmatic material everything that is heretical."[4] Every theology, then, must come to terms with the problem of heresy.

Schleiermacher understands heresy primarily as the intrusion of elements not contained in the central intuition of a faith and which, if taken seriously, threaten to contradict that faith and destroy its coherence in feeling. The essential or "natural" heresies for Christian faith are determined by its central intuition. Any doctrine that threatens the church's sense of redemption through Christ cuts the nerve of its confession.

There are two ways in which a heresy can arise: namely, (1) by an understanding of the human situation that renders the concept of redemption meaningless, or (2) by a view of Christ that makes it impossible for us to consider him the Redeemer. Thus every true heresy is either anthropological or christological in nature. The anthropological heresies are two: Any doctrine of man that sees him to be so dominated by evil as to be unworthy or incapable of redemption would destroy the hope at the heart of faith. This error the church has called Manichaeism. Conversely, any view of man that views sin so trivially that redemption is unneeded would likewise violate the Christian intuition. The church's name for this error is Pelagianism. Accordingly, the christological heresies are also twofold: "If Christ is to be redeemer . . . it is on the one hand necessary that he should enjoy an exclusive and peculiar superiority over all others, and on the other hand, there must be an essential likeness between him and all men, because otherwise what he has to impart could not be the same as what they need." [5] If the difference between Jesus and other men is judged so slight that he can no longer be conceived as Redeemer, but merely as a man like ourselves, we have fallen into the error of Ebionism. If, however, the difference between him and us is made so great that his relation to us vanishes and we cannot conceive how we can participate in the blessedness of his state, we fall into docetism. Thus a schematic representation becomes possible and the scope of Christian doctrine is established.

Anthropological Heresies	*Christological Heresies*
Manichaeism	Docetism
Pelagianism	Ebionism

The usefulness of this schematization lies partly in its negative character. Like the great classical definitions of Nicaea and Chalcedon, it preserves the integrity of Christian doctrine by setting limits. Not everything is Christian! But by so doing it establishes a broad range within which theological imagination can operate so long as it does not finally overstep the bounds established.[6] Also, like the classical creeds, its central concern is not speculative but religious—indeed, soteriological. It rules out every formulation which destroys in the believer the conviction that Christ has been manifest "for us men and for our salvation." [7]

While the church must deal with heresy for what it is, Schleiermacher advises caution and generosity toward the heretic. A man's faith is not identical with his expression of that faith and his deepest instincts may be more true than his doctrines. Indeed, if he chooses to remain with us, let him do so. If he is a heretic in heart as well as in doctrine, he will likely separate from us of his own accord.

3. The antithesis of sin and redemption must therefore be understood as accurately describing the Christian self-consciousness. If this is the case—if it is ecclesiastically valid—then it must evoke a sense of recognition in the believer. The

fact that it does tend to evoke response far more ungrudgingly than did Schleiermacher's doctrine of God shows that he is touching something basic in the Christian consciousness, and the strength of his subsequent anthropology and Christology argues that the forgiveness of sin through Christ is a central motif of that consciousness. But one must ask whether this picture is complete—whether in the quest for coherence and simplicity other intuitions equally fundamental have been over-looked. The description of Christian faith in terms of sin and redemption is certainly in keeping with the experience-oriented theology of Schleiermacher's Moravian past. Moreover, it reflects the preoccupation of the Protestant tradition and of Western Christianity in general. One who is familiar with pre-Augustinian Christianity, and especially with its overpowering sense of mortality and longing for victory over death, might well ask whether the Christian awareness includes the transition not only from sin to forgiveness but also from death to life. It may be that Schleiermacher's difficulty in knowing what to do with certain doctrines he recognizes to be deeply grounded in Christian faith—for instance, the resurrection of Christ and the "prophetic doctrines" relating to eschatology—derives from a too-narrow description of the Christian consciousness.

4. If the experience of redemption through Christ is the formal norm for Christian doctrine, what is the material norm? To what sources does the theologian turn for the "stuff" of doctrine? The answer must be the community of faith in which this experience has arisen and in which the theologian lives. Any doctrine set forth as true must find expression in the documents and confessions of Christian history, or it is immediately suspect. Thus all propositions which claim a place in an evangelical or Protestant theology "must approve themselves by appeal to Evangelical confessional documents," [8] and these, in turn, by appeal to the New Testament Scriptures.

Once again Schleiermacher's feeling for the historical church serves as a check against any temptation to allow the subjective self-consciousness to determine faith. The individual's experience arises from the rich substance of the community, past and present. While present experience can and must judge the past, so must it be judged by the past. One cannot with good conscience hold to a dogma that is uniformly rejected by the Christian past and finds no support whatsoever in the Scriptures. Schleiermacher, in actual practice, seems to maintain a dialectic among three norms for faith: Scripture, the traditions and creeds of the church, and the experience of the individual believer. These appear to be held in tension, each reinforcing, interpreting, and criticizing the other. More will be said below about the role of Scripture as a norm for faith.

SCHLEIERMACHER'S DOCTRINE OF MAN

The Christian doctrine of man must consider two aspects of the human situation, namely, (1) man's original righteousness by virtue of Creation and (2) his present situation as a result of the Fall. Failure to understand either will jeopardize the believer's awareness of redemption. But what can the doctrine of original righteousness mean, given the death of Adam? Certainly it cannot tell us about the natural origins of man as a part of the world.

Schleiermacher rejects a literal understanding of the Creation narratives, not only because such an understanding is scientifically untenable, but also because it does violence to their own clear religious intent. Insofar as the first three chapters of Genesis constitute a religious document, and not merely primitive science, they are concerned primarily with the meaning of human existence in relation to God. How little religious faith is concerned with origins except as those origins provide insights into present actualities and future possibilities! Therefore Schleiermacher denies that the doctrine of man's original righteousness refers to a golden age prior to the appearance of sin, for such is neither consistent with the evidence of science nor is it religiously significant. Rather, the doctrine of original righteousness affirms the essential goodness of man and repudiates the hopelessness inherent in all forms of naturalistic and anthropological cynicism. It affirms that there is nothing in man which is inherently hostile to God and to God-consciousness. The Creation narratives constitute the graphic rejection of Manichaeism by biblical faith. Whatever may be the depth of the God-forsakenness we call sin, it can never be ultimate; it can only be understood as a perversion of a more basic divine-human relation. It is the refutation of anthropological despair. The doctrines of Creation and of original perfection are seen to point not backward to what man was but forward to what he can hope to be. The doctrine of Creation is in the last analysis an eschatological doctrine. It affirms that nothing in all creation can finally destroy man's predisposition to God or his potential for God-consciousness.[9] Put simply, original perfection says that man is redeemable!

To describe man as essentially capable of fellowship with God and knowledge of God does not mean that he has within him the power to achieve such a fellowship. Schleiermacher does not intend to escape Manichaeism only to fall into the trap of an easy-going evolutionary Pelagianism such as characterized so many varieties of liberal theology later in the century. The blame for the faulty anthropology of later liberalism is often laid at Schleiermacher's door. Whatever the extent of his blame, it was certainly not his intention to overestimate man's capacity for growth into virtue. Such would amount to a doctrine of self-salvation, and Schleiermacher is too much the theologian of grace to make this error. There is indeed a potential for perfect God-consciousness in man, but it is *only* potential until it becomes actual in Jesus Christ.

The biblical drama of Creation and Fall steers a path between the anthropological heresies that would destroy the awareness of grace within us. Manichaeism is hopeless; Pelagianism is unrealistic, ignoring the persistence of man's evil and his inability to bring about reconciliation with God by his own resources. The primacy of created goodness means that sin can never be allowed an ultimate place in the system. It exists, so to speak, at a lower level of reality, since it is destined finally to be overcome by God, but it is not therefore of trivial significance. Alienation from God-consciousness cannot be conquered except by the divine grace made manifest in the Incarnation of Christ.[10]

THE DOCTRINE OF SIN

Schleiermacher's delineation of the doctrine of sin once again opens new ground for theology and sets directions for the nineteenth century. In accordance with the three forms all dogma assumes, Schleiermacher considers sin (1) as it arises in experience or as self-consciousness, (2) as it relates to God, and (3) as it affects the created order. In keeping with his method, the first is basic and the others are derived from it.[11] "We have the consciousness of sin," he writes, "whenever the God-consciousness which forms part of an inner state, or is in some way added to it, determines our self-consciousness as pain; and therefore we conceive of sin as a positive antagonism of the flesh against the spirit." [12] In other words, what we call sin is the experience of God accompanied by a sense of alienation or guilt. Sin is the state in which we find ourselves when we think of God, and it "hurts."

How does sin arise? Schleiermacher suggests that it can best be understood as the dominance of the flesh over the spirit. It begins with the arrest of the capacity for God-consciousness by the sensual self-consciousness. Both as a race and as individuals, we are aware of sin as "the power and work of a time when the disposition to the God-consciousness had not yet actively emerged in us." [13] This does not mean that every flaw must be accounted for or excused as an evolutionary or developmental "hangover." It does point, however, to our awareness that the God-consciousness struggling for expression in us is stifled by the flesh, the potency of which is felt as a determining presence. The flesh is *fact*; the God-consciousness by comparison is only potential. The "fallenness" of man points to this universal warring of the flesh against the spirit, not to a historical fall. This means that the condition of sinfulness represents less a rebellion against God than an incompleteness of creation awaiting its completion in Christ.[14] In the light of our experience of sin in the world, the following observations become possible:

1. *Sin and grace are inseparable.* Without God-consciousness there can be no awareness of sin, only animal sensuality. The awaking of our sense of God arouses in us a sense of the higher life we do not possess. The more acute the God-consciousness the more intense the awareness of sin. Witness Paul's agonizing cry, "I am the chief of sinners." This means that the emergence of sin-consciousness is a sign also of the grace of God.

2. *Sin cannot be outgrown or overcome by man.* Schleiermacher takes pains not to be misunderstood in this regard as advocating a naïve Pelagianism. Whatever its origin, sin will not disappear except by the redemptive or re-creative work of God. Man is the problem, not the answer.

3. *Sin is both an inheritance and a personal realization.* Schleiermacher is never more sensitive than in his analysis of the origins and forms of sin, particularly in relation to its social and personal dimensions. He speaks against those who would indict the individual and excuse society, or conversely, describe the individual as the helpless victim of an evil order. Neither corresponds to our experience, which is far more complex and dialectical. He writes: "We are conscious of sin as partly having its source in ourselves, partly . . . outside our own being." [15] We inherit it, both somatically and socially. This is the meaning of original sin. But we also affirm it and pass it on; original sin always issues in *actual* sin.[16] Sin then is both ours and society's. Society makes us sinful, but we also make society sinful. Thus we are allowed no facile Marxist reductionism ("It is the fault of the social order; men are good!") and no simple-minded pietism of a benign social order and sinful men.

It should be noted that Schleiermacher is here setting forth
a picture of corporate humanity that not only has profound biblical overtones, but has much in common with the understanding
of man and society informing twentieth-century Christian ethics. Can it be that the theologian often castigated as the hero
of introspective, individualistic liberalism is in fact the real
father of social Christianity? Walter Rauschenbusch thought
so.[17] The neoorthodox reader discovers with a sense of shock
that the words so often employed by the spokesmen of the social
gospel are not Rauschenbusch's, but Schleiermacher's. The latter writes, "Whether in fact, we regard [sin] as guilt and deed
or rather as a spirit and a state . . . [it is] *in each the work
of all, and in all the work of each;* and only in this corporate
character, indeed, can it be properly and fully understood." [18]

4. *The forms taken by sin may be relative to time and place,
but the fact of sin is universal.* Thus Schleiermacher addresses
a problem that has grown ever more acute with man's awakening historical consciousness. Although societies differ as to
what they consider to be sinful practices, they all agree in pro-
scribing some kinds of attitudes and behavior. Noting this fact,
we should be forewarned against leaping to the conclusion that,
because men disagree concerning the sinfulness of particular
actions, sin itself is an illusion created by social disapproval.
The *forms* of sin may be conditioned by society, but not the fact
of man's alienation from self and God.

5. *Natural evil can be comprehended as evil only from the
perspective of sin.* It is the anxiety and fear born of guilt that
makes pain and death evil, just as, once sin has been overcome
through grace, death itself can be accepted as God's good gift.
"Without sin there would be nothing in the world that could
properly be considered as evil." [19]

6. *Sin is properly defined in terms of relationship to God.*
Therefore all attempts to speak of sin and virtue quantitatively,
or to consider men as more or less sinful become meaningless.
Accordingly, all the ways in which sins have been differentiated
—appetition vs. act, unintentional vs. intentional, mortal vs.

venial—become suspect. "There is no meaningful difference of worth between men in regard to sin, apart from the fact that it does not in all stand in the same relationship to redemption." [20]

7. *Sin is finally and essentially an aspect of redemption.* Insofar as sin is real, and insofar as all things owe their existence to God, sin must have its source in God. In a system that affirms both God's sovereignty and his goodness, there is no way to avoid tracing evil and sin back to the author of the system. Any evasion of this fact ends up challenging either God's providence (and therefore his ability to conquer sin) or his love. Thus Schleiermacher affirms we must frankly confess that God is the author of sin. Yet we cannot regard him as the author of sin in the same sense that he is the author of redemption.[21] Sin can be instrumental but not ultimate. It corresponds positively to no attribute of God. The presence of sin and grace together in the Christian consciousness points to the fact that ultimately sin exists that it might be overcome by reconciliation.[22] Does this mean that sin is unreal for God? The answer must be yes if sin is understood as a power or a reality standing over against God and able to frustrate his redemptive activity. Sin is real as the precondition of reconciliation, but it is ultimately due to be taken up into God and rendered good.[23] Sin is finally, then, "God's strange work," intended to drive men into his arms. As we will see presently, this overpowering sense of the redemptive goodness of God leads Schleiermacher finally to espouse the idea of universal salvation. God may use sin and evil redemptively but never retributively, and never finally so.

REDEMPTION AND THE REDEEMER

The Christian Faith is a profoundly Christ-filled book, a fact the twentieth-century critique of Schleiermacher has often obscured. Indeed, the profound devotion to Christ that took root in Moravian pietism and found such beautiful expression in *Christmas Eve* achieves a remarkable dogmatic articulation in

Schleiermacher's *Glaubenslehre.* Niebuhr correctly observes that "it is not the religious feeling alone that endows the work with its significance, but equally important . . . is the position that the figure of Jesus Christ occupies."[24] It is regrettable that so little attention has been given to Schleiermacher's Christology. The following exposition can suggest only the most significant aspects of his attempt to come to grips with the work and person of the Redeemer.

CHRISTOLOGY FROM BELOW

The doctrine of Christ arises from the other side of the sin-redemption correlation. When God-consciousness is determined not as pain but as joy and blessedness, Schleiermacher says, the Christian finds that he must refer that transition in all aspects to the work of the Christ in him. It is the essence of the Christian confession that "we have fellowship with God only in a living fellowship with the Redeemer."[25] Schleiermacher is profoundly aware of the difficulties the modern Christian has in making sense out of the language of classical Christology. Thus if the church's faith in the Redeemer is to be sustained, it must subject itself to continual criticism, the aim of which is to rediscover the religious intentions behind the christological creeds and then to reconstruct dogma so as to express these inner intentions effectively for a new day.[26] The consequences of the Copernican revolution brought about by Schleiermacher are evident in his christological construction.

What were the religious aims to which classical Christology sought to give expression? The first attempts to understand the Christ and his function in the faith seem to foreshadow the formulations that became normative at the Council of Chalcedon. The apostolic church seemed to grasp from the beginning that redemption depended upon the unique manner in which Jesus had brought together divine healing and human need. His ability to help us consisted partly in the fact that he transcended the dilemma in which we lived. He was not—could not be—caught in the trap of mortality and sin. Thus the church did not blush to call him God. Yet his "transcendence" was but one side of his redemptive adequacy; his worth to men lay also in the immanence of that redemptive reality. He had to actualize redemption within human experience for it to be meaningful. He must be *God* with us, but he must also be truly God *with us men*.

Schleiermacher's formulation of the christological heresies reveals his faithfulness to the insights of Chalcedon. We must be able to feel toward Christ both "unconditional adoration" (*God* with us) and "brotherly comradeship" (God *with us*).[27] Ebionitic Christs fail on the first count, docetic Christs on the second. Schleiermacher believes, however, that the two-natures doctrine is no longer viable in its Chalcedonian form. There are philosophical reasons why this is so. The epistemological realism that shaped, in either its Platonic or Aristotelian forms, both classical and medieval thought no longer holds. Modern men are essentially sons of Hume and Kant, and terms like "*ousia*" or "nature" are meaningful only when their meaning is fixed in the context of the new epistemology. We see in Schleiermacher a sensitivity to the problems posed for traditional metaphysics and theology by the emergence of modern linguistic criticism. It will no longer do to speak of Christ as possessing "two natures in one person." "Nature" means quite simply what a thing is! To speak of a person as possessing two natures is either to describe a pathological condition or to use words without meaning.[28]

But the *theological* reason for revising the two-natures doctrine is the weightier: it is *nonexperiential*. We cannot approach Christ's divinity directly because we do not experience the divine nature of Christ in a direct way. This is why the older dogmatic procedures will not work any more. We cannot, for example, base our doctrine of Christ on an exposition of his divine status as the logos of God, and then, on the basis of his peculiar dignity, seek to understand what he has done for us. That is, we cannot really move from who and what he was to an understanding of what he has done. Christology "from above" has, since Schleiermacher, been largely replaced by a Christology "from below." Schleiermacher understands that if the classical affirmations about the nature of Christ are to be reaffirmed for the church today, it must be on the basis of what he has done for us. Christology for a new age must take a new tack— it must move not so much from Christ's person to his work but from his work to his person.

It is difficult to overemphasize the significance of this shift of order for almost all subsequent christological thought. Schleiermacher is, of course, merely making manifest a fact recognized by all scholars today. The church has always done Christology "from below." The apostolic church had at the beginning no Christology; it had only a tremendous experience with Jesus and the concrete fact of the church. It took five centuries for the christological doctrine of Chalcedon to take shape. What the church affirmed about Christ—who he was and what was his relation to God and man—was experiential; it was dictated by the reality of reconciliation that had come about through him. The recognition of the experiential foundations of all christological dogma opens the way, Schleiermacher feels, for a renewal of Christology.[29]

Thus Schleiermacher's Christology is Christology from below. This fact is not immediately evident to the reader, however. Schleiermacher does not feel it necessary to reverse the traditional organization, so his treatment of the person of Christ occurs first in *The Christian Faith*. As his exposition unfolds, however, his intent becomes increasingly clear. In the final analysis, the person and work of Christ are the same, since "the peculiar activity and the exclusive dignity of the Redeemer imply each other, and are inseparably one in the self-consciousness of believers."[30] But since we have no experience of his divine nature apart from our awareness of being redeemed by him and united thereby with God, the actual movement is from his work to his person. We experience forgiveness and grace in our hearts, we see his work manifest in the life of the church, and we are constrained to say that he is of God. Given the reality of redemption, "the dignity of the Redeemer must be thought of in such a way that he is capable of achieving this." [31] Schleiermacher's principle for christological reconstruction can be expressed thus: We must attribute to Christ no greater or no less dignity than is required by what he is to us and what he has done for us.

Now, it cannot be denied that this principle has a narrowing effect on Christology, for some traditional christological concepts may fail to meet this experiential criterion. Schleiermacher is nevertheless convinced that the resultant pruning will be a healthy and necessary consequence and that whatever remains of the traditional dogma will thereby have been placed on a more secure foundation. The reader of *The Christian Faith* will be impressed not by how much is lost by the application of Schleiermacher's experiential criterion, but by how much is retained and given fresh meaning.

THE PERSON AND WORK OF THE REDEEMER

What are we led to say of Christ, given his work in us? As has been suggested, most of the affirmations of traditional Christology find place in *The Christian Faith*. The following are of special interest and illustrate the procedure Schleiermacher employs in translating the ontological language of the creeds into confessional terms:

1. *The sinless perfection of the Redeemer.* The doctrine of the sinless perfection of Christ exemplifies the principle of attributing to him the dignity commensurate with his achievement. The church's belief in Christ's sinlessness is not based primarily on the moral character of Jesus as reflected in the Gospel accounts, impressive though it may be; rather, such a belief grows out of our awareness of him as Redeemer. In the *Speeches*, Schleiermacher had laid down the principle that that which mediates God must not itself require mediation. Since it is in fellowship with him that we have fellowship with God and in him that we find our less-than-ideal state of being trans-

formed, we must attribute to him the absolutely unbroken ideality we lack. To confess that he alone is Redeemer is to confess that he did not share our problem, and that for this reason he can help us. Belief in his sinless perfection does not rest upon a psychological examination of Jesus—such could never be conclusive, given the fragmentary evidence we possess —but on a theological analysis of the Christian self-consciousness.

2. *The divinity of the Redeemer.* Because of his mediation of redemption the church has called Jesus God. But what meaning can the language of divinity have, given the confessional and experiential nature of his Christology? Schleiermacher's answer is that the deity of the Redeemer must be thought of in terms of the "constant potency of his God-consciousness, which was *a veritable existence of God in him.*" [32]

It is, of course, the description of the deity of Christ in terms of God-consciousness that became one of the focal points of subsequent criticism. What is his meaning? Schleiermacher does not for a moment intend to reduce the dignity of the Redeemer or to diminish his unique status as the focus of revelation. Nor does he intend a Christ who is merely the wisest of men, who comprehends God more fully than the rest of mankind. Schleiermacher means that Jesus is uniquely the one in whom God dwells, but he is speaking confessionally, and only in a derived sense can his language be taken ontologically. [33] To understand the confession that Christ is God, one must again ask what he has done in us. Schleiermacher is once more moving from the work of Christ to his person. Furthermore, he is confident that in doing so he is following the path which led the apostolic church to the affirmation of Christ's deity. It was the church's experience that Christ existed in perfect unity with the Father. He was perceived as the one whose fellowship with God was unmediated and so unbroken that he was able to say, "I and the Father are one." The apostles felt there was no blasphemy in representing the Redeemer as saying, "He that hath seen me hath seen the Father." What was present in the best of men only in a fragmentary and anticipatory way was present in Jesus in unsurpassable perfection. Thus they confessed, "He is God!"

But is it enough to describe Christ's oneness with God in terms of God-consciousness? Much of the discomfort subsequent interpreters have felt with Schleiermacher's Christology grows out of the fear that such a description is too denatured and insubstantial to meet the needs of Christian confession. Schleiermacher would merely ask what other meaning could be given to deity in a man. To give this relational understanding of deity ontological status would serve only the purpose of emphasis. It would say no more about the perfect and inalienable fellowship between the Father and the Son, "for to ascribe to Christ an absolutely powerful God-consciousness and to attribute to him an existence of God in him are exactly the same thing." [34] However, any attempt to "ontologize" his deity, that is, to construct a speculative doctrine on the basis of this confessional truth, would generate the same insoluble difficulties with which traditional Christology has so long been saddled. Indeed, to think of Christ's divinity in terms of his perfect fellowship with the Father is the *only* way in which we can conceive of God as being in a man without violating the integrity both of his manhood and of God.

3. *The work of Christ in redemption.* Christ relates to Christianity not merely as founder but as Redeemer. That is to say, he is not merely the revealer but the one in whom redemption becomes a reality. He is not to be understood as an example of what every man, given the proper incentive, can become. It is our experience that redemption could not have happened apart from its realization through Christ. How then does he redeem us? Schleiermacher commences his treatment of the work of Christ with the following famous proposition: "The Redeemer assumes believers into the power of his God-consciousness, and this is His redeeming activity." [35] This is to say that through him we experience fellowship with God. To know Christ is to know God; to be bound in love to the Christ is to enter into an

inseparable unity with the Father. The God-consciousness that we achieve through Christ is, for Schleiermacher, far more than cognitive. It is, indeed, a kind of intimate union in which we share with him, and by his agency, fellowship with the eternal God. Through Christ, who lives in perfect oneness with the Father, we are bound into an inseparable relationship in which we also "know" him.[36]

4. *The uniqueness and finality of the Redeemer.* Perhaps the most persistent misunderstanding of Schleiermacher has been in reference to the place Christ holds in Christian faith. Can it be said that Jesus is in any sense unique as a possessor and revealer of God-consciousness? If he is unique, is his uniqueness merely that of a historical founder? Can others be in a similar way unique mediators of God to men in other histories? What's more, do we, once we have been awakened to spiritual life through his mediation, continue that spiritual existence on our own? Is he the great "discoverer" whom we remember with gratitude, but of whom we then become independent? And, if he is the great discoverer, then despite his pivotal historical importance for us, could he not, at least in principle, be equalled or surpassed by others yet to come?

If any of the above questions can be answered affirmatively, then the charge often leveled against Schleiermacher that his Christ is merely the loftiest of religious discoverers and not truly mediator of a unique and final redemption would be substantiated. Then we could perhaps speak, as some have done, of Schleiermacher's "many Christs"; and the reproach of Brunner that many mediators is equivalent to no mediator at all would have to be taken seriously.[37] But so to understand Schleiermacher's intentions is an error, one that has resulted partly from reading him in the light of later liberal Christologies. The justice of such a reading, on the other hand, lies in the fact that the deficient Christology of the *Speeches* probably influenced later nineteenth-century christological thought more deeply than did part two of *The Christian Faith.*

But the mature Schleiermacher is emphatic in rejecting any

such view of Christ, since it would contradict the consciousness of redemption. The activity of Christ must be comprehended, he insists, as unique not merely in degree but in kind, for "if his influence is only of the same kind as others, even if it is ever so much more complete and inclusive, then . . . the salvation of mankind would be a work common to Him and the others . . . and there would be, not one Redeemer over against the redeemed, but many, of whom one would be only the first among those like him." [38] Such a view, he feels, would violate both the Christian awareness of sin and the consciousness of divine grace by assuming Christ did no more than we in principle can do. Furthermore, such a redeemer could be—and one might expect him to be—surpassed by others; and this violates the deepest intuitions of the Christian life, namely, that the whole of our existence is "in Christ." Our relation to God is not merely instituted by Christ but remains dependent on him. He writes: "Now, if we live in the Christian fellowship, with the conviction which is common to all Christians, that no more perfect form of the God-consciousness lies in front of the human race, then any thought that another can be redeemer or that we might one day pass beyond him would clearly mark the end of the Christian faith.[39]

CHRIST AND THE NEW HUMANITY

It is clear, then, that Schleiermacher intends the universal redemptive significance of Christ to be taken seriously. His saving activity does more than create a new awareness, it brings about a new situation, moving us to inquire about the cosmic dimensions of the Christ. In so doing we encounter Schleiermacher's understanding of atonement. One might ask how Christ can be unique in the way described above and still be man. How can he be free from sin, since sin is both biologically and socially rooted? Does he not, in some decisive manner, have to come from outside the order of nature and of fallen humanity? But would not such a Christ be a miracle, and would this not shatter Schleiermacher's understanding of the created order?

Schleiermacher's answer is that Christ is indeed a miracle, but not an "absolute miracle." He is a miracle in the sense that his sinless perfection is inconceivable apart from the operation of divine grace. He does indeed come from outside the problem. What he was and is cannot be explained exhaustively by past human experience. By bringing a new element to the human situation, he changes that situation decisively so that what, prior to him, was only potential becomes in him actual. Christ's work is not to be conceived merely in revelational terms, so that what has always been the case is made manifest in him; it is genuinely redemptive, in that it changes the order of things. He is the second Adam, who introduces a new element into human history. He is the "absolute *novum*" (Moltmann) in whom the qualitatively new is actualized. He does more than to reveal God, he brings about the "New Being" (Tillich). This genuine newness can only be seen as the miraculous re-creative activity of God.

Christ is not a miracle, however, if by this is meant a violent rupturing of the fabric of nature. Schleiermacher, despite his deep sense of the integrity of the cosmos, is far from being a captive of the narrower Newtonianism that had fixed itself on many of the sons of the Enlightenment and is still to be encountered today. Nature and history are not to be conceived as such a closed order that nothing genuinely new is possible. A closed mechanistic cosmos would be inconsistent with the dynamic interrelatedness of life. But whatever is conceived as genuinely new must in a larger sense be an expression of the character and purpose of the cosmos as the creation of God. It may be new in that it cannot be explained exhaustively by past history, but it must be the actualization of what was potential from the beginning.

This is true of the Christ. He is miracle but not complete miracle. He comes to us as the "happy surprise," as the one who demonstrates that perfect God-consciousness and perfect humanity do not contradict but require each other. What seems existentially unthinkable is shown in Christ to be real, namely, man and God in a perfect unity which, far from nullifying humanity, allows it for the first time to become what it can be. Redemption is now seen to be the completion of Creation.[40] Christ is the second Adam through whom it becomes possible for men for the first time to become truly men. This is Christ's atoning work: to announce, exemplify, and actualize in the world the new humanity in which, through him, we participate.

Thus also light is shed on the nature of the divine-human unity in the Redeemer, since Christ's humanity can be affirmed without sacrificing the fullness of the divine presence in him. The human person in Christ is not to be thought of as pre-existent *logos* but is brought into being in the Incarnation. The drive of the divine creativity is toward personhood, and the personhood of the man Jesus is fully actualized by virtue of the fullness of the God-consciousness in him. Perfect manhood and perfect God-consciousness require each other, and the creative act of God in Christ is itself the fullest expression of human existence. The problem vanishes: to achieve perfect God-consciousness is to achieve the fullest and deepest selfhood conceivable. So also in Christ our humanity is not diminished but actualized. Thus Niebuhr is led to call Schleiermacher's view of atonement "christomorphic."[41]

EVALUATION

Whatever one's final evaluation of Schleiermacher's Christology, the reader cannot fail to be impressed by the venturesome and creative nature of his work. He is not afraid to challenge boldly the doctrinal past; yet he does so without falling victim to the reductionism of some later liberals. He seeks to do justice to all the central insights of traditional Christology, and it is remarkable how many of these he is able to incorporate into his thought.

While the contemporary reader may not accept fully his restructuring of traditional concepts, neither does he feel that Schleiermacher does serious violence to the substance of chris-

tological faith. Even when Schleiermacher cannot easily incorporate an element of tradition into his Christology, he is
loath to cast aside anything that is deeply grounded in the
Christian past and in the New Testament. An example of this
reticence is Schleiermacher's treatment of the doctrine of
Christ's resurrection. Unable to discover any real connection
between the resurrection and the experience of redemption
(possibly because, as has been noted, he gives scant attention to
the "death-life" motif),[42] he nonetheless believes the resurrection took place. The Christian church cannot take seriously the
suggestion that the apostles, on whose testimony the church
rests, could have been so deceived.[43]

One major question is likely to persist in the mind of the
reader, whatever his reaction to Schleiermacher's Christology
considered in itself. What is the relation, if any, between the
doctrine of the Redeemer and the doctrine of God set forth in
the first part of the system? It is evident that Schleiermacher's
sensitive and sometimes eloquent Christology has been carried
on with little reference to the doctrine of God. What has been
said, or implied, about God and his activity in redemption has
far transgressed the limits placed on God-talk by the feeling of
absolute dependence. Either the theology of part two exists in a
kind of parenthesis, so that it finally speaks about "nothing
real in God" but only in the manner of our perceiving, or the
feeling of redemption requires affirmations about God and
about his relation to the world that could never be posited on
the basis of the feeling of absolute dependence. Once again the
reader is forced to ask whether the seemingly contradictory affirmations of the first and second parts of the system can be
brought together in a way that will preserve the coherence of
The Christian Faith.

THE REALM OF REDEMPTION

Fellowship with Christ gives rise to a new quality of existence in the believer and creates a new community among be-

lievers. Through the work of grace a new corporate life of the
redeemed and sanctified is brought into being. There is little
place in Schleiermacher's thought for the lonely discipleship;
his theology is thoroughly church-centered. It is possible here
to highlight only a few aspects of this soteriology and ecclesi-
ology that are especially suggestive for future Protestant
thought:

1. *Regeneration and sanctification.* Regeneration and sanctification occur essentially within the new corporate community,
and consist in the ever-greater dominance of God-consciousness
over the whole person. Since the divine activity is "person-
forming," this process does not diminish selfhood but enriches
it. Sanctification is never complete in the world; the old identity
persists, so that, as in Luther, the believers remain at the same
time sinners and justified. However, sin in the life of the regen-
erate is no cause for despair, because the awareness of God's
grace and forgiveness is the solid ground of hope. "Since they
are always being combatted, the sins of those in the state of
sanctification always carry their forgiveness with them and
have no power to annul the divine grace of regeneration." [44]
The security of the believer lies in the abiding grace of God,
not in his own good works. Nevertheless, faith drives toward
social expression and toward good works. Good works cannot
qualify regeneration and justification [45] but regeneration gives
rise to works, for they are the natural effects of faith, in that
faith generates a sensitive concern for others and a feeling of
unity with other creatures that participate in the divine love.

2. *Election.* Schleiermacher's treatment of the doctrine of
election is remarkably sensitive and perceptive. He understands
its importance to Protestant thought and to any theology that
takes grace seriously; yet he fully understands the dilemma
that the doctrine of dual election poses for the modern conscience. He concludes that the time has come for the church to
reject the concept of dual decree, since such a concept shatters
the sense of racial unity generated in us by God's grace. If we
hold to double election, then we must conclude that a large

portion of the race was never intended for the divine reconciliation, and this would be a retreat into a Gnostic discrimina-
tion between types of men, namely, those created for grace and
those for destruction.[46] Furthermore, taken seriously, such a
doctrine would destroy our sense of blessedness in God. If we
accept the damnation of those for whom God's grace has
taught us to care, can we still say "God is love"? Schleiermacher concludes that finally we have two choices concerning
the doctrine of election: we can attribute the two decrees to
divine capriciousness and endanger faith itself, or we can affirm that the disparity of God's dealing with men is only ap-
parent and that ultimately all men will be taken up into his
love.

Thus Schleiermacher espouses universal salvation as the
necessary concomitant of the experience of reconciliation. If
redemption is corporate, and if it gives rise to a sense of the
unity of mankind, then it must be concluded that the divine
election includes the whole human race on the basis of God's
good pleasure.[47] "There is," he writes, "a single divine foreordination, according to which the totality of the new creation
is called into being." [48] This new creation cannot be exclusive,
lest the nerve of faith be severed. Indeed, Schleiermacher anticipates the concept of racial election that figures prominently
in the thinking of Karl Barth, for finally "God regards all men
only in Christ" and we have no other way open to us but to
take foreordination to blessedness "quite universally." [49]

3. *The role of the Scriptures.* Schleiermacher's formal treatment of the Scriptures occurs in his discussion of the "Essential and Invariable features of the church." [50] Once again his
sensitivity to the past and to the current needs of faith is
evident. Schleiermacher is fully aware of the problems raised
by historical-critical study of the Scriptures. He is not a pol-
ished biblical critic, but subsequent biblical scholarship has to
a large degree followed the way opened by his views. He seeks
to steer a course between a rigid biblical positivism that closes
its eyes to the facts and a supercilious indifference to the Scrip-

tures. Thus he points the way to a clear-eyed and honest biblical scholarship which nevertheless keeps its roots in a warm,
confessional Christianity.

The New Testament Scriptures for Schleiermacher, belong
not to the *bene esse* of the church but to its *esse*—that is, not
merely to its well-being but to its essence. Considered historically, they represent but one instance of the apostolic witness.
As a permanent reflection of Christ's prophetic activity, however, they constitute the most direct source of apostolic faith
and make of the New Testament the norm for all subsequent
expressions. No dogma can be considered Christian unless it is
at least compatible with the witness of the Scriptures. Their
normative power does not rest on historical primacy alone; the
authority of the New Testament for the Christian church is an
experienced fact. The church has had no choice in the matter
because the Scriptures have, so to speak, forced themselves
upon the community of faith.

It must be made clear that in the final analysis faith validates
Scripture. This is why rational arguments for the reliability of
Scripture are persuasive only to those who stand already within
the faith. If the Christian heart does not affirm the authority of
Scripture it has none.[51] The authority of Scripture is, in contemporary terms, existential. It is the church's confession that
the New Testament is an adequate and reliable authority for
Christian faith. Such a definition of the Scripture's role, Schleiermacher feels, liberates the believer from the dominance of
narrow biblicism. He can affirm, for example, that not all parts
of the Scriptures are equally normative, for not all speak with
equal power to the central motif of redemption. Furthermore,
not every ramification of faith or every expression of the gospel
has to be contained in the Scriptures from the first. Indeed, if
faith is a living thing, then the richness of its understanding
should grow with new experiences in the world. Schleiermacher
seems to propose the idea, common to Catholic Christianity,
that while the essential substance of faith is given, new dogmas
may become explicit only with the passage of time.[52] But this

fact must not, he warns, lure us into a naïve evolutionary pattern of thinking, so that we allow thought and life to be substituted for the Scriptures as the norm for faith.

At all events, the church must remember that with reference to both Scripture and theological tradition, the final criterion is christological, because the ultimate and *original* revelation, upon which the church's very existence rests, is not the Scriptures but the Christ. To speak of the sufficiency of the Scriptures is to say that "through our use of Scripture the Holy Spirit can lead us into all truth, as it led the Apostles and others who enjoyed Christ's direct teaching. So that if one day there should exist in the Church a complete reflection of Christ's living knowledge of God, we may with perfect justice regard this as the fruit of the Scripture." [53]

V. An Assessment of Schleiermacher's Accomplishment

BEYOND THE CHASM

Any attempt to assess the significance of Schleiermacher's accomplishment must deal with the difficulty manifest repeatedly in the foregoing chapters—the struggle between two seemingly essential elements of his theological system, namely, the feeling of absolute dependence and the experience of redemption through Christ. Schleiermacher seems to assume that these two sources of doctrine are compatible and complementary. It has been argued above that a real tension exists between what is demanded by the one (God's absolute independence, his freedom from change, temporality, etc.) and what is implied by the other (God's involvement in the realm of created being, his redemptive activity, his "relativity" to the object of his creativity and love). In the body of the work the relation between the general and the Christian self-consciousness is never adequately clarified. As a result, Schleiermacher seems to have not one theology but two. Part one is a theology of divine causality or "omnipotence" while part two is a theology of redemptive love. As has been seen, the problem is not of Schleiermacher's making, but is the result, at least in part, of faith's attempt to affirm both God's sovereignty and his love. But if Schleiermacher cannot point the way beyond this inherited dilemma, not only will the coherence and fruitfulness of his system be threatened, but his value for subsequent Christian thought will be imperiled.

The difficulty of collating the two elements of his theology lies partly in the manner in which Schleiermacher employs the concept of the feeling of absolute dependence. Schleiermacher rightly locates one essential element of the religious intuition in the feeling of absolute dependence insofar as it points to the character of God as sovereign or provident. It expresses confessionally the sense that God, to be worthy of worship, must somehow exemplify both causation and control. But when employing the feeling of absolute dependence as a criterion for God-talk, Schleiermacher seems to lose sight of its confessional character. Thus he falls into the trap of extrapolating from it not confessionally, as his own method requires, but *logically*, by inversion. Absolute dependence may imply absolute independence but providential trust does not, and it could be well argued that the latter is the real substance of the religious feeling to which the idea of omnipotence points. That is to say, the feelings of absolute dependence and omnipotence are to be understood as "explanatory doctrines" that seek to express in language the religious intuition from which they spring, not speculative a prioris from which the character of God and the world can be unfolded deductively.

Because he fails to distinguish the religious and the speculative meaning of divine omnipotence, for example, Schleiermacher seems to see no way to affirm the former without undermining the dynamism of God implied in the Christian self-consciousness. Had he been genuinely confessional in his understanding of the religious intuition and untrammelled by the philosophical and linguistic concerns especially evident in part one, he might have made the important discovery that divine providence and sovereignty need not be absolute to fulfill the requirements of religious faith.

But to criticize Schleiermacher in this way is to take advantage of hindsight. He cannot be blamed for being unaware of the contemporary critique of absolutist theism by thinkers like Berdyaev, Whitehead, and Hartshorne. Indeed, the effort of these men and others like them to uncover the religious meaning or essence in the traditional language of omnipotence would have been unthinkable before Schleiermacher. Nonetheless, Schleiermacher's insistence on the logical convertibility of the feeling of absolute dependence appears to create a chasm down the middle of the system.

Schleiermacher is aware of the problems created for biblical faith by a God whose dynamic participation in creation seems threatened by his own perfection. Schleiermacher's discomfort is revealed in his treatment of the divine omniscience. After all that has been said, it is somewhat surprising to discover an almost Bergsonian passage in which he suggests that

> if the term . . . omnipotence is not to be thought of as a "dead" force, the same result would be reached by the expression "absolute vitality." And this pair, inwardness and vitality, would be just as exhaustive a mode of presentation and one perhaps even more secure against all admixture of alien elements.[1]

Here he seems to reveal dissatisfaction with the absolutist tendencies in his own formulation, and he seems to strain forward in search of a way to transmute the infinite character of the divine nature into vitalistic terms. However, the tension between the absolute and relational dimensions of the divine creativity is never resolved in the body of the system, so as to make the redemptive theology of its second part compatible with God's absolute causality.

GOD AS LOVE

In a remarkable third section of *The Christian Faith*, Schleiermacher attempts at last to come to grips with the problem described above. This concluding section is in effect an appendix demanded by the need to articulate more adequately the two parts of the dogmatic. Here he confronts the question raised earlier whether, in the final analysis, what can be said about God is determined by the feeling of absolute dependence or the feeling of redemption, and his answer reemphasizes his basic stance as a theologian of the Christian community. Whatever the problems for interpreting his doctrine of God, Schleiermacher affirms that, in the last analysis, the essence of the divine nature and activity must be understood from within the realm of redemption. Therefore he inquires about the divine attributes that relate to redemption. But to ask this question means to consider the significance of the dominant affirmation of historic Christianity, namely, that God is love. The attempt of Schleiermacher to bring together the divine omnipotence and the divine love is not without difficulties, but it does suggest the possibilities for development inherent in his theology. Briefly stated, the argument by which Schleiermacher seeks to bridge the chasm and to unite the theology of absolute dependence and the theology of divine love runs as follows:

While omnipotence says something necessary and real about God, by itself it is merely abstract, lacking any specific content, much as if one were to call a person consistent without specifying the character in that consistency—generous or miserly, childish or mature. To speak of God as omnipotent says little. Power per se is morally neutral, simply fact; and a God who is merely sovereign has little religious value. So are all the metaphysical attributes abstract and religiously unavailable. Schleiermacher concludes that God as "cause" is incomplete. If God is to have a quality that makes him worthy of worship, an attribute must be found that describes the concrete essence always manifest in his omnipotence. *This is not given in the feeling of absolute dependence; it is given in its fullness only in Christ.* Schleiermacher writes,

As regards the attributes which we arrived at in the first part of this work, they made then no claim to rank as such designations of the Divine essence that they could be substituted for the name "God." Even though we explain omnipotence as the attribute in virtue of which all finite things are through God as they are, while we certainly in that case posit the divine act in its entirety, it is *without a motive*, and therefore . . . wholly indeterminate in character.

Indeed, he adds, "belief in God as almighty and eternal is nothing more than that shadow of faith which even devils may have." [2] It is, rather, in the experience of the divine love that what was abstract, tentative, and incomplete is rendered whole. So it is that omnipotence receives its religious character from love. Schleiermacher writes that "while we certainly might venture to say that God is loving omnipotence or omnipotent love, yet we must admit that in the first of these forms as much as in the second, love alone is made equivalent of the being or essence of God." [3] Indeed, from the perspective of redemption it becomes evident that not only the metaphysical attributes but also the moral and religious attributes of God (such as holiness, justice, and wisdom) merge finally in the divine love. In one of the most eloquent passages in *The Christian Faith* Schleiermacher seeks to bring the demands of divine power into harmony with redemptive love:

We cannot say that God in Himself is justice and holiness; for neither of these attributes can be conceived apart from a relation to evil as well as to the antithesis between evil and good. . . . Hence the action of these attributes separately from the others is exclusively limited to a certain sphere, and it is only when we cancel this separation and resolve them into those attributes which we are now discussing as the result of the second half of our exposition, that they are recognizable as divine attributes at all. So that what was formerly considered as the work of divine holiness and justice is now properly . . . reckoned as part of the work of redemption. Thus both of these attributes, like the others, merge for us in the divine love, this last viewed solely in its preparatory manifestations; and the divine love is holy and just love inasmuch as essentially it begins with these preparatory stages; in the same way it is almighty and eternal love. Love and wisdom alone, then, can claim to be not mere attributes but also expressions of the very essence of God.[4]

THE LEGACY OF SCHLEIERMACHER

It remains for a word to be said regarding Schleiermacher's contribution to the modern theological mind. To refer to him as the father of modern theology is not to suggest that he is the sole source of the insights on which subsequent Christian thought was to develop. Yet more than any other, he brought to clear focus the nature of the challenge faced by modern theology and the directions faith would have to move in meeting this challenge. The extent to which Schleiermacher's theological achievement has contributed to the method and substance of nineteenth- and twentieth-century theology remains impressive. What are the chief elements of Schleiermacher's legacy to the contemporary theology? Only a few of the most significant can be mentioned.

1. *The consciousness of a changed world.* Schleiermacher represents theology and faith come alive to the new world. He was aware that the stable past was no more and that nothing would ever again be as it had been. This sense of a world in dynamic flux was new in Schleiermacher's time, but it appears to be a permanent dimension of modern life. Schleiermacher was the first theologian of major stature to accept the dynamism of the modern world view and to seek to do his work as a theologian from that perspective.

2. *The necessity for a dialogue between theology and the world.* Schleiermacher saw himself as a Christian believer but also as a citizen of the modern world, and he understood that he had a commitment to both. For him the church shared the situation of the world and had no choice but to participate fully in the life of the world. Schleiermacher knew that the theologian must stand within the theological circle, and that his fundamental loyalty must be to the church and to Christ, but he also knew that the circle of faith stands within the larger circle of the world. Thus the theologian must live always in tension between these two foci of his being. He is never al-

lowed to withdraw from the life of mankind and exist in comfortable isolation from intellectual and ethical challenge. Neither is he to become so much a man of his age that he surrenders the stance of the believer.

This creative tension of faith and life was exemplified in Schleiermacher's own career. He sought to accept the attitudes of modern life and the methods of modern scholarship whenever good sense and good morals required it. He sought therefore real intellectual and critical honesty. Yet he had no intention of effecting the kind of surrender to narrow rationalism that was to characterize some later forms of liberal Christianity. Schleiermacher accepted in general the validity of science and philosophy but at the same time sought to bring to it a healthy criticism when it exceeded its bounds or became doctrinaire. The attempt to be responsible both to faith and to the world has, in varying degree, characterized most subsequent theology.

3. *The establishment of a positive attitude toward society.* The attempt at rapprochement described above implies an affirmative attitude toward society. Schleiermacher was by no means an uncritical yea-sayer, but he realized that society is not, per se, the enemy of faith, and that the church must recognize and sympathetically appropriate the wholesome, creative, and human elements in the secular order. Again he set the mood for later liberalism, a mood which was by no means lost even in the modified world-contempt of early crisis theology.

Such an affirmation of society implied the social commitment of faith. Schleiermacher's understanding of the social dimensions of sin, and his sense of the racial consciousness to which faith in Christ gives rise, helped to open the way to a more socially responsible Christianity. Schleiermacher's own social activism took the form of patriotism and has been criticized as leading to the kind of naïve "Culture-Christianity" into which German liberalism fell in the twentieth century, therefore requiring the wholesome corrective supplied by Barth and the crisis theologians. Nonetheless, the social conscience

of modern Christianity owes much to Schleiermacher's view
of the church as a community of redemption seeking to actualize the human brotherhood implicit in the experiences of creation and reconciliation.

4. *The adaption of Christian faith to historicism.* It was at
the beginning of the nineteenth century that the implications
of the modern historical consciousness for faith began to be
evident. Schleiermacher was the first major theologian to seek
to understand those implications and to develop a theology
that would speak to historical man. While relativism posed
problems, it also helped free Christian faith from dogmatism
and from slavish loyalty to elements of the past that were no
longer viable. As has been seen, the acknowledgment of the
historical character of theology opened the way to a new
humility and graciousness among theologians and laid the
foundations for modern theological ecumenicism. It also provided a principle for criticizing every pretense to absolute
authority—theological, philosophical, or political—because
the historical relativity of all truths means that none can claim
finality or demand unconditioned loyalty. This fact was to
provide Karl Barth with his weapon against Hitler, Reinhold
Niebuhr with his critique of culture, and Paul Tillich with his
"Protestant principle."

The acceptance of the historicity of faith meant acknowledging the changing character of the church's theology and of the
church itself. Schleiermacher again opened the way to the
future by demonstrating that the church and the theologian
can live creatively with change. His own willingness to re-
formulate old creeds and revise old dogmas was an expression
of his confidence that faith does not require the kind of
finality of expression that destroys its dynamism or its open-
ness to the future. Yet he was able to accept the fact of change
because of his conviction that the reality out of which faith
arose was not transient or variable. Thus the acceptance of the
reality of change provided Schleiermacher with the perspective
and incentive to seek a new kind of basis for faith. If a contemporary Christianity is to maintain continuity with its past,

then there must be permanent truths, values, and experiences underlying its changing formulations. His sense of the historical continuity of faith led him to examine every dogma in an effort to discern the stable reality of which it is the expression. His search for the essence within the doctrines of faith provided a characteristic motif of later liberal theology. The attempt of the modern theologian to extract the religious or experiential-existential meaning of dogmatic and creedal expression reflects this motif.

5. *The acceptance of the experiential or existential character of theology.* Schleiermacher found himself in a world that no longer accepted traditional or "received" authority. Thus he felt constrained to ask whether the theologian's task could be redefined in experiential terms. Since Schleiermacher's time, and to no small degree by his influence, the experiential principle has become firmly established. Whether Schleiermacher was correct that all of his theological affirmations arose from the feeling of absolute dependence or from the feeling of redemption is beside the point. What has been criticized as his subjectivism is in fact the underlying assumption of both liberalism and neoorthodoxy, namely, that the final criterion of the truth of any proposition is experience. This is surely as true of the "theologies of the Word" as it is of Bultmann and his disciples, and likely will remain the underlying presupposition of all future theology.

6. *The defining of the task of theology in confessional terms.* Karl Barth is said to have changed the title of his systematic theology from *Christian Dogmatics* to *Church Dogmatics* in order to underline the fact that the theologian exists to serve the worshiping community. However, the realization that theology arises from, gives voice to, and serves the needs of the church is nowhere given more graphic expression than in Schleiermacher. What he formally proposed in the *Brief Outline on the Study of Theology* he exemplified with great faithfulness in his scholarship and life. No theologian—not even Barth—has taken the confessional nature of the theological task more seriously than Schleiermacher. In this respect he

must be considered the forerunner of the strong confessionalism
that characterizes neo-Protestant theology in our own time,
though not of the tendencies to isolation and obscurantism that
often accompany the modern form.

7. *The beginning of a certain wholesome pragmatism regarding "hard metaphysics" or speculation.* For Schleiermacher, the focal point of theological life was the positive
community of faith, and theology's primary task was a prag-
matic one, namely, the strengthening of the church's life in
worship and mission. From his own emphasis on the community as prior to dogma, to Ritschl's "nonmetaphysical historicism," to Harnack's and Rauschenbusch's search for an
undogmatic Christianity, modern theology has seen itself as
the servant of the practical life of faith. The same nonspecu-
lative pragmatism is reflected in many theologians of the
present century, for example, Reinhold Niebuhr, Rudolf Bultmann, and Dietrich Bonhoeffer. In more recent decades, theologies of social revolution (Third World, black, and female
theologies) share Schleiermacher's theological pragmatism but
not his systematic rigor or comprehensive perspective.

8. *The beginning of a persistent Christocentrism.* It is interesting to observe the degree to which nineteenth- and twentieth-century theology has been obsessed with the figure of
Jesus. Whether as the "historical Jesus" of the later Ritschlians,
neoorthodoxy's "Christ of faith," Tillich's bringer of The New
Being, or William Hamilton's "man for others," the christological preoccupation of modern Christian thought has been
remarkable. Schleiermacher's personal piety from his earliest
Moravian days was profoundly oriented toward the figure of
the Redeemer. Although he quickly forsook the simplistic
soteriology of Niesky, he never lost his commitment to Christ
as the center of the Christian faith and as the unique revealer
of the divine love. To the extent that subsequent Christian
thought has felt compelled always to come to terms with the
figure of Jesus Christ, it has once again borne witness to the
legacy of the author of *The Christian Faith.*

Notes

INTRODUCTION

1. Princeton, N.J.: Princeton Theological Seminary, 1966.

CHAPTER I

1. Descriptions of the eighteenth-century background of modern thought are numerous. A brief treatment that stresses aspects of that background especially relevant to theological development is in James C. Livingston, *Modern Christian Thought from the Enlightenment to Vatican II* (New York: Macmillan, 1971), chaps. 1–3.

2. *The Question of God: Protestant Theology in the Twentieth Century*, trans. R. A. Wilson (New York: Harcourt Brace Jovanovich, Harvest Books, 1969), p. 11.

3. Richard R. Niebuhr, *Schleiermacher on Christ and Religion* (New York: Charles Scribner's Sons, 1964), p. 76 n. All further references to Niebuhr in the present study are to Richard R. Niebuhr unless otherwise stated.

4. See Niebuhr's treatment of Schleiermacher's hermeneutics, ibid., pp. 72 f.

5. See Schleiermacher, *The Christian Faith*, ed. H. R. Mackintosh and J. S. Stewart, with an introduction by Richard R. Niebuhr (New York and Evanston: Harper and Row, Harper Torchbooks, 1963), sec.

17, pp. 83 f. See also Schleiermacher, *Brief Outline for the Study of Theology,* trans. Terrence N. Tice (Richmond, Va.: John Knox Press, 1966), sec. 9, p. 21.

6. It is sometimes suggested that the markedly "Christian" character of *The Christian Faith* does not reflect the author's personal theology, but that it is a scientific and descriptive treatment of Christian theology by a writer who does not himself stand within the Christian faith. Schleiermacher's insistence on the confessional nature of theology as well as the clearly confessional tone of both the *Speeches* and *The Christian Faith* renders such a view untenable. Indeed, his eloquent description of the true preacher-theologian in the *Brief Outline* (secs. 4–17, pp. 20–23) applies happily to his own work.

7. *Brief Outline,* sec. 9, p. 21.   8. Ibid., p. 124.

9. *The Christian Faith,* sec. 17, pp. 83 f.

10. To be sure, "system" to Schleiermacher does not mean a closed, deductive system that makes no allowance for the dynamism of life and thought. It means, rather, that thought, while arising from the church's faith, must nonetheless strive for an expression that is both internally coherent and intelligible. In theology, *system* refers to the church's thought "at a given time" (*The Christian Faith,* sec. 19, p. 88), and remains always open to new insights and experiences. It is interesting that Paul Tillich, whose theology most resembles Schleiermacher's among twentieth-century theologians, found it necessary to defend in a similar way his own use of *system* (see *Systematic Theology* [Chicago: University of Chicago Press, 1957], II, 3–5).

11. Schleiermacher, *On Religion: Speeches to Its Cultured Despisers,* trans. John Oman, with an introduction by Rudolf Otto (New York: Harper and Brothers, Harper Torchbooks, 1958), p. 40.

12. Martin Redeker, *Schleiermacher: Life and Thought,* trans. John Wallhausser (Philadelphia: Fortress Press, 1973), p. 17.

13. Schleiermacher, *Soliloquies,* trans. Horace Leland Freiss (Chicago: Open Court, 1957), p. 74.

14. Ibid., pp. 74–75. It is difficult to exaggerate the importance of this passage for modern Christianity. Schleiermacher here finds the basis for a distinction between theological formulations and the living religious experience from which they grow, thus laying down the axiom that different forms of religious expression can arise from a common religious awareness. It is difficult to imagine how modern ecumenical Christianity could have arisen without this distinction.

15. Redeker, *Schleiermacher,* p. 24.

16. Schleiermacher, *Christmas Eve: Dialogue on the Incarnation,*

trans. Terrence N. Tice (Richmond, Va.: John Knox Press, 1967).

17. See Niebuhr's comments in *Christ and Religion*, pp. 255 f. See also Redeker, *Schleiermacher*, p. 10.

18. Although Kant represented a turning point and a new departure, to call him "the decisive influence," as Freiss does in his introduction to the *Soliloquies* (p. xxxii), is to obscure the substantial differences from Kant present almost from the beginning and the increasing extent to which Schleiermacher transcended the limits of the critical philosophy. The mature Schleiermacher was not "neo-Kantian" in the same way that Ritschl was.

19. See Arthur v. Ungern-Sternberg, "Die Begegnung von Theologie und Philosophie bei Schleiermacher in seiner Reifezeit," *Zeitschrift fur Theologie und Kirche* 41 (1943) :292.

20. Redeker, *Schleiermacher*, pp. 25–34.

21. The romanticism of Johann Gottlieb Fichte stressed the creative activity of the Ego, which goes out from itself to shape its world. The fundamental fact of the universe is free Spirit, and the world is a creation of Spirit, rather than its source, as the materialist would hold. The purest expression of Spirit, then, and the moral obligation of the self is continual striving, against everything that would restrain or limit it, for the achievement of true freedom and perfect understanding. It is this Promethean striving and cocksure self-affirmation that Schleiermacher finds to be so foreign to the spirit of true religion. See Niebuhr's remarks in *Christ and Religion*, pp. 33 f. See also Redeker's comments on the relation of Schleiermacher to Fichte, pp. 29 f.

22. See, for example, Richard B. Brandt, *The Philosophy of Schleiermacher: The Development of His Theory of Scientific and Religious Knowledge* (New York: Harper and Bros., 1941), pp. 217 f. Cf. ibid., p. 236. Cf. also Karl Barth, *Protestant Thought from Rousseau to Ritschl*, trans. Jaroslav Pelikan (New York: Harper and Bros., 1959), pp. 328–29.

23. See Niebuhr's treatment in *Christ and Religion*, pp. 29 f. Gerhard Spiegler, in *The Eternal Covenant* (New York: Harper and Row, 1967), makes more of the methodological significance of Plato than of the substantive influence (see chap. 3).

24. Schleiermacher, *The Christian Faith*, sec. 4, p. 12.

25. *Schleiermachers Sendschreiben über seine Glaubenslehre an Lücke.* ed. Hermann Mulert (Giessen: Alfred Topelmann, 1908).

26. See Niebuhr's introduction to *The Christian Faith*, p. xiii.

27. Ibid., pp. xiii–xiv. See also Terrence Tice's translation of Schleiermacher's *On Religion: Addresses in Response to Its Cultured*

Critics (Richmond, Va.: John Knox Press, 1969), p. 24, for Tice's comments concerning the distinction between true and false objectivism in the epistemology of Schleiermacher.

CHAPTER II

1. *Protestant Thought in the Nineteenth Century* (New Haven and London: Yale University Press, 1972), pp. 4–8.

2. John Oman's pioneering 1893 translation has recently been supplemented by Terrence Tice's excellent new translation. Tice's version is much superior in clarity but occasionally sacrifices the force and nobility of the Oman version. All references to the *Speeches* are to the Tice version except where specifically indicated otherwise.

3. Rudolf Otto, Introduction to *Speeches* (Oman).

4. The phenomenological methodology of the *Speeches*, is, of course, not identical with that of twentieth-century phenomenology as derived from the thought of Edmund Husserl. It could, however, be said to anticipate Husserl and the later phenomenologists in significant respects, for example, in its attempt to circumvent a narrow positivism by carefully circumscribing its own goals and truth claims. In common with the phenomenologists, Schleiermacher asks the hearer to pay attention to the phenomena as experienced, without prior ontological commitment, before judging how they can be interpreted in the larger scheme of things. Insofar as Schleiermacher is the first major theologian consciously to adopt a phenomenological methodology, he clearly points out the path to be followed by Otto, Sabatier, Bergson, and, more recently, Tillich and Hartshorne.

5. Redeker, *Schleiermacher*, p. 36. Here we find expression of the desire manifested in the *Soliloquies* to penetrate behind appearances and to discern "the inner nature of things" (see pp. 74–75).

6. Redeker rejects the analysis that the *Speeches* is "a psychological account of the religious life in terms of the psychological categories of that day" (p. 35). He is, of course, right that it is not *merely* that. Schleiermacher does indeed employ the "faculty psychology" of his time, but in the end he transcends it. As we shall see, religious feeling is no psychological faculty but the fundamental awareness of which the faculties are functional expressions.

7. *Speeches*, p. 54.   8. Ibid., p. 79.

9. This is especially true with regard to the word *feeling* ("*Gefuhl*"). In the first edition of the *Speeches* it was supplemented by the term *Anschauung*, usually translated *intuition*, a term better suited in

many respects to describe the fundamental awareness that unites all particular thoughts, acts, and feelings. However, in later editions of the *Speeches*, the use of *Anschauung* declines and in *The Christian Faith* almost disappears—perhaps, as Redeker suggests, because Schleiermacher feared it would be confused with the "intellectual intuition" of Idealism (Redeker, p. 40). Tice chooses to translate it "perspectivity," since he understands religion to be, according to Schleiermacher, "a vital inner perspective on the whole scheme of things which is centered in the process of attaining true humanity, and is sustained in deeply personal feeling" (*Speeches*, p. 10). Intuition, with this broader meaning, will be retained in the present treatment.

10. *Speeches* (Oman), p. 41.   11. *Speeches*, p. 82.
12. Ibid., p. 79.   13. Ibid., p. 93.
14. Ibid. (Oman), pp. 49–50.
15. Redeker, *Schleiermacher*, p. 42.   16. *Speeches*, p. 82.
17. Ibid., pp. 182–83.   18. Ibid., p. 194.
19. Ibid. (Oman), p. 122.   20. Ibid., p. 182.
21. It is happily no longer necessary to defend Schleiermacher on the charge of Spinozism, a charge he himself sought to refute in the later editions of the *Speeches*. On the nature and significance of Spinoza's influence, see Niebuhr, *Christ and Religion*, pp. 90–92. See also Hefner, p. 93 n., and Redeker, *Schleiermacher*, pp. 43–44.
22. Schleiermacher's protest against pantheism in the *Speeches* is not dissembling. He feels the difference between his position and pantheism is substantive. The clear formulation of that difference awaits *The Christian Faith*. See especially sec. 8, postscript 2.
23. *Speeches*, pp. 114–15.
24. Schleiermacher appears at this point to stand closer to Luther than to Calvin. Calvin's unswerving commitment to the principle that the finite is not capable of the infinite and his resulting tendency toward docetism stand in contrast to Luther's monophysite inclinations, and this difference is to be felt in the area of Christology and especially in the controversy over the sacraments. Luther's espousal of the dogmas of the communication of idioms and of the ubiquity of Christ's humanity both express his "pansacramental" tendency. It is Schleiermacher's belief that there is no necessary hostility between the divine and the human that makes possible both his Christology and his "christomorphic" doctrine of the atonement (see Niebuhr, *Christ and Religion*, pp. 210–48). It is also this pansacramental tendency of Schleiermacher that in large measure arouses the Calvinist horror of Karl Barth. Conversely, it helps account for the theological kinship between Schleiermacher and the Lutheran Tillich.

25. *Speeches*, p. 48.   26. Ibid., p. 148.

27. See above, chap. 1, pp. 38–39.

28. Insofar as the concept of the absolute is a human formula, it is also anthropomorphic. Here Schleiermacher seems to anticipate Whitehead's doctrine that abstractions, while real, are so in a secondary way and are derived from primary reality. Schleiermacher's sense that the concrete is primary and the conceptual derived from it requires of him that he become a "critic of abstractions" in the Whiteheadian sense. See Alfred North Whitehead, *Science and the Modern World* (New York: Free Press, 1967), chaps. 3 and 4. See especially pp. 58–59.

29. *Speeches*, p. 149. Emphasis added.

30. Ibid.   31. Ibid., p. 277.   32. Ibid., p. 208.

33. Ibid., pp. 208–209.

34. Ibid., p. 276. See also Schleiermacher's eloquent description of the preacher and his role, ibid., pp. 210–11.

35. Ibid., p. 305.   36. Ibid. (Oman), p. 238.

37. Ibid., p. 305.   38. Ibid., pp. 280–81.

39. Ibid. (Oman), p. 223.

40. *The Christian Faith*, sec. 17, 2. See below, p. 93.

41. *Speeches*, p. 308.   42. Ibid.   43. Ibid., p. 309.

44. Ibid., pp. 308–309.   45. Ibid., pp. 309–310.

46. Ibid., p. 311.   47. Ibid., p. 315.   48. Ibid., p. 316.

49. See John Calvin, *The Institutes of the Christian Religion*, trans. Henry Beveridge (Grand Rapids, Mich.: Wm. B. Eerdmans Publishing Company, 1957), bk. 2, chaps. 12–17.

50. *The Christian Faith*, sec. 93, 1.   51. *Speeches*, pp. 317 f.

52. *The Christian Faith*, sec. 93, 2.

CHAPTER III

1. See Niebuhr, *Christ and Religion*, pp. 28–30, 77–78, on the relation of Schleiermacher's Plato studies to his method. See also Spiegler, *The Eternal Covenant*, pp. 43 f., especially as it applies to Schleiermacher's philosophical method.

2. *Brief Outline*, p. 21.   3. *The Christian Faith*, secs. 2–3.

4. Ibid., sec. 3, 3.   5. Ibid., sec. 3, 3; sec. 4.

6. Ibid., sec. 3.   7. Ibid., sec. 4.   8. Ibid., sec. 33.

9. Ibid., sec. 4, 4.

10. Schleiermacher's point here is similar to Tillich's when the latter insists that the term *ultimate concern* must have both a subjective and an objective focus. If the believer concludes that what concerns him ul-

timately has no reality and corresponds to nothing "out there," in the universe, then its capacity to bear the weight of ultimate concern collapses (see *Dynamics of Faith* [New York: Harper and Brothers, 1957], p. 10). This is why Tillich insists in his *Systematic Theology* that "that which concerns us ultimately must belong to reality as a whole; . . . otherwise, it could not concern us" (p. 21). It is not surprising, then, when Tillich reveals that the concept of ultimate concern that serves as the formal criterion of his theology is his own reformulation of Schleiermacher's concept of absolute dependence (p. 42).

11. Schleiermacher's comments on pantheism are sensitive and perceptive. Pantheism is, in the first place, a speculative ideal unrelated to any actual historical community and does not spring from the religious affections. Indeed, pantheism, when analyzed, always tends to become either "some variety or form of theism"—struggling with the inadequacies or difficulties of naive theistic expression—or "simply and solely a disguise for a materialistic negation of theism" (*The Christian Faith*, sec. 8, postscript 2). Insofar as it is the former, it is a cry for a "better theism." Until dogmatics and philosophy provide a more adequate way of speaking of God and the world, Schleiermacher concludes, "we cannot avoid an oscillation between formulas, on the one hand, which approach to the identification of the two, and formulas . . . which go near to putting them in opposition to each other" (ibid., sec. 46, 2). Schleiermacher seems to defend himself successfully against the charge of pantheism. The persistent question in his doctrine of God is not pantheism but personalism. (See Niebuhr's introduction to *The Christian Faith*, p. xx.)

12. See C. W. Christian, "The Concept of Life after Death in the Theology of Jonathan Edwards, Friederick Schleiermacher and Paul Tillich" (Ph.D. dissertation, Vanderbilt University, 1965), pp. 205–206.

13. Richard R. Niebuhr, "Schleiermacher on Language and Feeling," *Theology Today* 27 (July 1960) :161.

14. It is difficult to resist the force of Schleiermacher's argument here. One cannot help asking, however, if there is yet another step, especially in view of the secularization of modern life and the emergence of the "death-of-God" theologies in the present century. Many gods, one god, *no* god?

15. *The Christian Faith*, sec. 11.   16. Ibid., sec. 11, 4.

17. Ibid., sec. 15.   18. Ibid., sec. 17.   19. *Speeches*, p. 232.

20. *The Christian Faith*, sec. 16.   21. Ibid., sec. 19.

22. Ibid., sec. 19, 2.   23. Ibid., sec. 32.   24. Ibid.

25. Niebuhr, "Schleiermacher on Language and Feeling," p. 161.

26. See, for example, Schleiermacher's handling of God in relation to temporality (sec. 52) and omniscience (sec. 55), the latter being translated as the "absolute spirituality of the divine omnipotence." The difficulty Schleiermacher feels in handling "personal" attributes of God is in part due to the normative role played by the feeling of absolute dependence in shaping the doctrine of God. Indeed, he explicitly warns the reader that the hymnic and sermonic way of speaking reflected in the divine attributes must be carefully guarded, because "it may easily be led into saying something about the Infinite Being which would contradict the antithesis contained in self-consciousness and represent the Infinite Being as dependent on the finite" (sec. 35, 2).

27. Ibid., sec. 35.

28. For comments on the relation of Schleiermacher's thought to that of Kierkegaard, see Niebuhr, *Christ and Religion*, especially pp. 72 f.

29. *Speeches*, p. 88.

30. See, for example, the discussion of "Signs and Wonders" in Bernhard W. Anderson, *Understanding the Old Testament* (Englewood Cliffs, N.J.: Prentice-Hall, 1957), pp. 43–44, for a Schleiermachian exposition in the context of biblical theology. Compare also the "pan-sacramentalism" of Paul Tillich.

31. See Schleiermacher's treatment of the methods of arriving at the divine attributes, sec. 50, 3.

32. Thus aseity, or independence, is a "shadow picture" of omnipotence and therefore of absolute causality (sec. 54, postscript).

33. *The Christian Faith*, sec. 1, 2.

34. Ibid., sec. 50; see sec. 51, 1 also.   35. Ibid., sec. 51.

36. Ibid., sec. 37, 1.   37. Ibid., sec. 170, 1.

CHAPTER IV

1. *Speeches*, p. 241. See above, p. 69.

2. *The Christian Faith*, sec. 11.   3. Ibid., sec. 11, 4.

4. Ibid., sec. 21.   5. Ibid., sec. 22, 2.

6. The healthy latitude Schleiermacher allows for theological formulation contains a somewhat wry comment on what might be called "theological perspective," and a warning to the heresy hunter. Insofar as we remain within faith, we always stand somewhere on the line between each pair of opposite determinations. But if we stand near to one heresy—say, Pelagianism—the man in the middle appears to us, by foreshortening, to stand at the other extreme. So all who are doce-

tists in their hearts interpret any reference to a full humanity in the Christ as Ebionism (sec. 22, 3).

7. This phrase, which occurs in both the Nicene and Chalcedonian formulas, expresses the soteriological concern underlying the trinitarian and christological struggles of the Patristic period. The time is now happily past when the creedal formulations were dismissed as the intrusion of speculative concerns into the simple religion of the apostles. For a brief but excellent treatment of the subject, see Maurice Wiles, *The Making of Christian Doctrine* (Cambridge: University Printing House, 1967).

8. *The Christian Faith*, sec. 27.   9. Ibid., secs. 59, 60.

10. Ibid., sec. 65, p. 270.   11. Ibid., sec. 64.

12. Ibid., sec. 66.   13. Ibid., sec. 67.

14. Niebuhr is essentially correct in his observation that the terms *redemption* and *redeemer* are not the most appropriate ones for expressing Schleiermacher's view of Christ's work, since he substitutes for the concept of redemption that of the completion of the creation (see *The Christian Faith*, p. xix). It should also be pointed out that Schleiermacher's use of the term *flesh* has no Manichaean implications. Schleiermacher does not mean by the flesh the physical body, but the whole man viewed from the perspective of his antagonism to God.

15. *The Christian Faith*, sec. 69.

16. Ibid., sec. 73.

17. See Walter Rauschenbusch, *A Theology for the Social Gospel* (New York: Macmillan, 1917, Abingdon Apex ed.), p. 27.

18. *The Christian Faith*, sec. 71, p. 288.

19. Ibid., sec. 75, 3.   20. Ibid., sec. 74.

21. Ibid., secs. 79, 80.   22. Ibid., sec. 80.

23. Ibid., sec. 81, p. 338.

24. Introduction to *The Christian Faith*, p. xviii. Niebuhr's remark that Schleiermacher is not really a christocentric thinker can be misunderstood. It is true that he is finally concerned not with the Christ but with the God whom he mediates. It is difficult, however, to discover a Christian theologian of stature who is not theocentric in the same sense. Schleiermacher is, for instance, not less christocentric or more theocentric than Luther or Barth.

25. *The Christian Faith*, sec. 91.   26. Ibid., secs. 95–96.

27. Ibid., sec. 96.   28. Ibid., sec. 96, pp. 392–93.

29. The extent to which much contemporary Christology is "functional," stressing the religious "value" of Christ (Ritschl) and frequently showing indifference to speculative reconstruction, suggests the

degree to which subsequent theology has followed the path set out by Schleiermacher.

30. *The Christian Faith*, sec. 92.   31. Ibid., sec. 93, 1.

32. Ibid., sec. 94, emphasis added.

33. It has been argued above that Schleiermacher is at heart a realist, and that his strictures against speculation must be carefully understood. He does not for a moment doubt that the feeling of absolute dependence puts one in contact with the really real, or that to experience redemption in Christ is to really experience God, but any attempt to speak of "being itself" must be experientially grounded. Metaphysics is therefore a descriptive science. It seeks not to talk about a world that transcends finite experience but of the invariable and essential qualities of being that are manifested in experience. Schleiermacher seems therefore to understand metaphysics as the search for principles of utmost generality given in experience, an understanding shared in various ways by Heidegger, Whitehead, and Husserl.

34. *The Christian Faith*, sec. 94, pp. 386–87.

35. Ibid., sec. 100. Compare also sec. 88.

36. The Johannine character of this language has not escaped comment. See Niebuhr's remarks in *Christ and Religion*, pp. 64–65, as well as in the introduction to *The Christian Faith*, p. xix.

37. Emil Brunner, *The Mediator* (Philadelphia: Westminster Press, 1957), chap. 1.

38. *The Christian Faith*, sec. 92, p. 374.

39. Ibid., sec. 93, pp. 377–79. He writes: "Now, if we live in the Christian fellowship, with the conviction which is common to all Christians, that no more perfect form of the God-consciousness lies in front of the human race, . . . the thought either of desire or ability to go beyond Christ marks the end of the Christian faith."

40. Ibid., sec. 94, p. 389.   41. *Christ and Religion*, pp. 210–248.

42. Ibid., sec. 99. See comments above, p. 111.

43. *The Christian Faith*, sec. 99, 2.   44. Ibid., sec. 111.

45. Ibid., sec. 112.   46. Ibid., sec. 120, postscript, p. 558.

47. Ibid., sec. 120.   48. Ibid., sec. 119, p. 550.

49. Ibid., sec. 120, postscript, p. 560.   50. Ibid., sec. 127.

51. Ibid., sec. 128.   52. Ibid., sec. 129, p. 596.

53. Ibid., sec. 131, 2.

CHAPTER V

1. *The Christian Faith*, sec. 51, 2.   2. Ibid., sec. 167, 2.

3. Ibid., sec. 167, 1.   4. Ibid., sec. 167, 2.

Selected Bibliography

I. WORKS OF SCHLEIERMACHER

Much of Schleiermacher's sizable literary output remains unavailable in English. However, his major religious and theological writings are now accessible in good translations. The following are recommended:

Schleiermacher, Friedrich D. E. *Brief Outline of the Study of Theology.* Translated by Terrence N. Tice. Richmond, Va.: John Knox Press, 1966.

————. *The Christian Faith.* English translation of the second German edition. Edited by H. R. Mackintosh and J. S. Stewart. Edinburgh: T. and T. Clark, 1948. Available in two volumes with an introduction by Richard R. Niebuhr. New York and Evanston: Harper and Row, Harper Torchbooks, 1963.

————. *Christmas Eve: Dialogue on the Incarnation.* Translated by Terrence N. Tice. Richmond, Va.: John Knox Press, 1967.

————. *On Religion: Addresses in Response to Its Cultured Critics.* Translated by Terrence N. Tice. Richmond, Va.: John Knox Press, 1969.

————. *On Religion: Speeches to Its Cultured Despisers.* Translated by John Oman, with an introduction by Rudolf Otto. New York: Harper and Bros., Harper Torchbooks, 1958.

————. *Soliloquies.* Translated by Horace Leland Freiss. Chicago: Open Court Publishing Company, 1957.

II. BOOKS AND ARTICLES ABOUT SCHLEIERMACHER

Ackert, Paul Herman. "The Religious Philosophy of Schleiermacher with a Translation of his *Reden über die Religion.*" Ph.D. dissertation, University of Pittsburgh, 1957.

Baillie, Donald M., trans. *The Christian Faith in Outline.* Edinburgh: Henderson, 1922.

Barth, Karl. "Brunners Schleiermacherbuch." *Zwischen den Zeiten* 2 (1924):49–64.

———. "Das Wort in der Theologie von Schleiermacher bis Ritschl." *Die Theologie und die Kirche* (1928):190–211.

———. "Liberal Theology: Some Alternatives." *Hibbert Journal* 59 (1961):213–19.

———. "Schleiermacher." In *Protestant Theology: From Rousseau to Ritschl.* Translated by B. Cozens and H. Hartwell. New York: Harper and Bros., 1959.

Benson, John E. "Schleiermacher's Hermeneutics." Ph.D. dissertation, Columbia University, 1967.

Braham, Ernest G. "The Theology of Schleiermacher." *London Quarterly Review* 152 (1929): 100–103.

Brandt, Richard. *The Philosophy of Schleiermacher.* New York: Harper and Bros., 1941.

Brandt, Richard B. *Philosophy of Schleiermacher: The Development of His Theory of Scientific Knowledge.* Westport, Conn.: Greenwood Press, 1968.

Brunner, Emil. *Die Mystik und das Wort: Der Gegensatz zwischen moderner Religionsauffassung und christlichem Glauben dargestellt an der Theologie Schleiermachers,* vols. 4, 8. Tübingen: 1924; 2d ed., 1928.

———. *Erlebnis, Erkenntnis und Glaube.* Tübingen: 1921; 1923.

———. "Karl Barth's Alternatives for Liberal Theology: A Comment." *Hibbert Journal* 29 (1961):319.

———. *The Mediator.* Translated by Olive Wyon. Philadelphia: Westminster Press, 1947.

Chan, David Tak-Yan. "The Critique of Schleiermacher's Theology by Emil Brunner and Karl Barth." Ph.D. dissertation, Edinburgh, 1959.

Chapman, J. Arundel. *An Introduction to Schleiermacher.* London: Epworth, 1932.

Diller, Elliot Van N. "Revelation and Mythology: Friedrich Schleiermacher versus Johann Grohmann." *Crozer Quarterly* 25 (January 1948):12–26.

Dilthey, Wilhelm, ed. *Aus Schleiermachers Leben in Briefen,* vols. 3–4. Berlin: Reimer, 1861–63.

———. *Schleiermachers Philosophie und Theologie.* Edited by Martin Redeker. Berlin: DeGruyter, 1966.

Dupre, Louis. "Toward a Reevaluation of Schleiermacher's Philosophy of Religion." *Journal of Religion* 44 (April 1964) :97–112.

Flowers, Harold J. "Schleiermacher." *Baptist Quarterly* 7 (1934): 49–59.

Funk, Robert W., ed. *Schleiermacher As Contemporary.* New York: Herder and Herder, 1970.

Gage, W. L. "Schleiermacher As a Man." *New Englander* 21 (July 1862) :427–45.

Groskreutz, Donald A. "The Pastoral Theology of Friedrich Schleiermacher." *Religion in Life* 28 (1959) :557–66.

Harvey, Van A. "A Word in Defense of Schleiermacher's Theological Method." *Journal of Religion* 42 (July 1962) :151–70.

Kraeling, Emil G., "Schleiermacher and the Old Testament." In *The Old Testament Since the Reformation,* pp. 59–67. New York: Harper and Bros., 1955.

Krapf, Gustav-Adolf. "Platonic Dialectic and Schleiermacher's Thought: An Essay Towards the Reinterpretation of Schleiermacher. Ph.D. dissertation, Yale University, 1953.

Loew, Cornelius R. "The Christology of Friedrich Schleiermacher." S.T.M. thesis, Union Theological Seminary, 1942.

Lucke, Friedrich. "Reminiscences of Schleiermacher." In *Brief Outline of the Study of Theology,* by Friedrich Schleiermacher, trans. William Farrar. Edinburgh: 1850.

Mackintosh, Hugh Ross. *Types of Modern Theology.* New York: Chas. Scribner's Sons, 1937.

McGiffert, Arthur Cushman. "The Theology of Crisis in the Light of Schleiermacher." *Journal of Religion* 10 (1930) :362–77.

McClymont, A. W. "The Theology of Friedrich Schleiermacher: Some Characteristic Elements." *Evangelical Quarterly* 20 (1948) :108–24.

Mehl, Paul Frederick. "Schleiermacher's Mature Doctrine of God As Found in the *Dialektik* of 1822 and the Second Edition of *The Christian Faith.*" Ph.D. dissertation, Columbia University, 1961.

Moore, W. L. "Schleiermacher As Prophet: A Reckoning with His View of History." *The Springfielder* 32 (Winter 1969) :7–14.

Niebuhr, Richard R. Introduction to *The Christian Faith,* by Friedrich Schleiermacher. New York: Harper and Row, Harper Torchbooks, 1963.

———. *The Meaning of Revelation.* New York: Macmillan, 1941.

————. *Resurrection and Historical Reason.* New York: Chas. Scribner's Sons, 1957.

————. *Schleiermacher on Christ and Religion: A New Introduction.* New York: Chas. Scribner's Sons, 1964.

————. "Schleiermacher on Language and Feeling." *Theology Today* 17 (July 1960) :150–67.

————. "Schleiermacher: Theology As Human Reflection." *Harvard Theological Review* 55 (January 1962) :21–49.

Oman, John. Review of Chapman's 1932 Schleiermacher book. *Journal of Theological Studies* 34 (1933) :213–14.

————. "Schleiermacher." *Journal of Theological Studies* 30 (1929) : 401–405.

Otto, Rudolf. *The Idea of the Holy.* New York: Oxford University Press, 1923.

Pannenberg, Wolfhart Ulrich. "Schleiermacher." *Encyclopaedia Britannica*, vol. 20, pp. 72–73.

Platt, Frederic. "Schleiermacher as Preacher." *London Quarterly Review* 159 (January 1934).

Redeker, Martin. *Schleiermacher: Life and Thought.* Translated by John Wallhausser. Philadelphia: Fortress Press, 1973.

Reist, J. S. "Continuity, Christ, and Culture: A Study of F. Schleiermacher's Christology." *Journal of Religious Thought* 26, no. 3 (Autumn 1969).

Rust, Eric C. *Positive Religion in a Revolutionary Time.* Philadelphia: Westminster Press, 1970.

Sandbach-Marshall, M. E. "Study of Schleiermacher's Conception of God." *Church Quarterly Review* 102 (April 1926) :68–97.

Schweitzer, Albert. *The Quest of the Historical Jesus.* New York: Macmillan, 1948.

Spiegler, Gerhard Ernst. "Between Relativity and Absolutism: A Study of Problematic Dimensions in the Dialektik and Dogmatik of Friedrich Schleiermacher." Ph.D. dissertation, University of Chicago Divinity School, 1961.

————. *The Eternal Covenant: Schleiermacher's Experiment in Cultural Theology.* New York: Harper and Row, 1967.

Sponheim, Paul Ronald. "The Christological Formulations of Schleiermacher and Kierkegaard in Relation to Fundamental Options in Divergent Strands in Their Discussions of God and Man." Ph.D. dissertation, University of Chicago Divinity School, 1961.

Stewart, H. L. "Schleiermacher, Ritschl, Barth: A Sequence." *Hibbert Journal* 50 (1951) :10–17.

Streetman, Robert F. "Friedrich Schleiermacher's Doctrine of the

Trinity and Its Significance for Theology Today. Ph.D. dissertation, Drew University, 1975.

Sykes, Stephen. *Friedrich Schleiermacher.* Richmond, Va.: John Knox Press, 1971.

Thoman, George Hasson. "Revelation, Faith, and Doctrine: A Study Based on the Theology of John Calvin, Friedrich Schleiermacher, and Karl Barth." Ph.D. dissertation, Vanderbilt University, 1961.

Tice, Terrence N. *Schleiermacher Bibliography with Brief Introductions, Annotations and Index.* Princeton: Princeton University Press, 1966.

————. "Schleiermacher's Theological Method: With Special Attention to His Production of Church Dogmatics." Th.D. dissertation, vols. 1–2, Princeton Theological Seminary, 1961.

Verheyden, Jack C. "Christology and Historical Knowing: A Study Based on the Thought of Friedrich Schleiermacher and the New Quest of the Historical Jesus." Ph.D. dissertation, Harvard University, 1968.

White, Frank T. "Systematic Theological Principles of Friedrich Schleiermacher and Paul Tillich." Ph.D. dissertation, Columbia University, 1966.

Wilburn, Ralph Glenn. "The Role of Tradition in Schleiermacher's Theology." *Encounter* 23 (Summer 1962):200–215.

————. "Schleiermacher's Conception of Grace, in the Light of the Historical Development of the Doctrine of Grace." Ph.D. dissertation, University of Chicago, 1945.